Human Rights

EQUAL ACCESS

HUMAN RIGHTS

EQUAL ACCESS

Safeguarding
Disability Rights

written by
Gregory J. Walters

Rourke Corporation, Inc.
Vero Beach, Florida 32964

Cover design: David Hundley

Library of Congress Cataloging-in-Publication Data
Walters, Gregory John, 1956-
    Equal access: safeguarding disability rights / by Gre-
gory John Walters.
        p.   cm. — (Human rights)
    Includes bibliographical references and index.
    Summary: Discusses the rights of persons with disabil-
ities, including equal access to buildings, public facilities,
and houses and equal opportunity in education, employment, and transportation.
    ISBN 0-86593-174-7 (alk. paper)
    1.   Handicapped — Government   policy — United
States — Juvenile literature.   2. Handicapped — Legal
status, laws, etc. — United States — Juvenile literature.
    [1.   Handicapped — Government   policy.   2.
Handicapped — Legal status, laws, etc.]   I. Title.   II.
Series: Human rights (Vero Beach, Fla.)
HV1553.W35   1992   92-11523
362.4'046'0973 — dc20   CIP
                                                 AC

Contents

Human Rights

EQUAL ACCESS

Chapter One

What
Are
Disability Rights?

Persons with disabilities are persons who experience some degree of physical, mental, or emotional limitation. They include persons who are deaf and hearing-impaired, persons who are deaf and blind, and persons with mental retardation, learning disabilities, physical disabilities, birth defects, vision impairment, emotional impairment, or mobility impairment. Persons with disabilities do not like to be labeled "handicapped" or "disabled." They want to be respected as human beings: for what they are able to do, not for what they are not able to do.

Persons with disabilities possess the same rights to life, liberty, and the pursuit of happiness as others. They have these rights because they are human beings with innate dignity. All human rights, and their corresponding duties, flow directly and spontaneously from the dignity of the human person. Human dignity and human rights are universal to all human beings and must not be violated.

The right to life, liberty, and the pursuit of happiness requires the defense of other rights, such as equal access to buildings, public facilities, houses, apartments, and shops; equal access in education, in employment, in housing, and in transportation. Negative attitudes toward persons with disabilities form the greatest obstacle to their achieving these rights. While great strides have been made toward implementing the rights of persons with disabilities, discrimination, apathy, and separation persist to this day.

A History of Separation

The policy of separating or segregating persons with disabilities from the mainstream of society was common from the 1920's until the early 1970's. For example, in 1925, one of the first car manufacturers in the United States made its workers with amputations wear artificial limbs. The company did this not because it was concerned about persons without arms or hands. The company did this, rather, because it did not want other workers to see a person with physical limitation. The company's managers believed that a physical impairment should be hidden from view.

The system of public education for most of the twentieth century has separated persons in a similar fashion. Schools have not been designed to help persons with disabilities. The traditional attitude was that public schools should not educate persons with disabilities. The major viewpoint was that they should be separated from society and educated in special hospitals or schools.

Persons in wheelchairs have often not been able to get a room in a hotel until quite recently in history. The excuse given was that the hotel did not want to be responsible for the person in case of a fire. While such overt discrimination has changed in recent years, some people still do not want to be reminded of the needs and rights of persons with disabilities. Instead, they would prefer that persons with disabilities be secluded in institutions, that they remain "second-class citizens," or that they be kept out of sight.

The separation of persons with mental retardation has resulted in some of the most serious violations of basic human

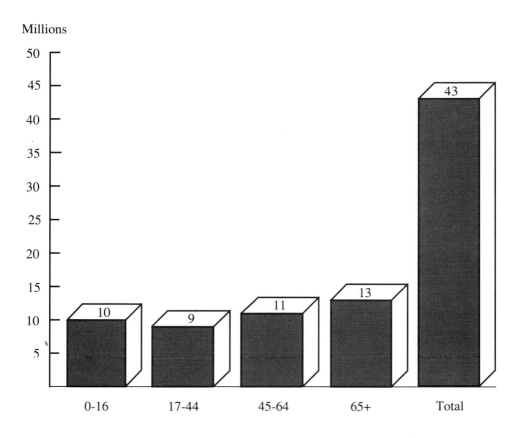

Millions

rights. In the mid- to late 1800's, for example, states routinely institutionalized mentally ill and mentally retarded persons in a "state lunatic asylum." The reasons given were that mentally retarded persons could not make proper decisions or that they posed a danger to themselves or others. Persons with mental illness or mental retardation were often sterilized involuntarily (without their knowledge or agreement). This practice was legal in twenty-nine states by 1934.

In 1956, Willowbrook State School on Staten Island, New York, was a home for mentally retarded children with a population of 4,478. Two doctors, Saul Krugman and Joan Giles, collected twenty-five thousand blood specimens from more than seven hundred patients. These doctors deliberately infected some of the incoming children with a hepatitis virus then prevalent at Willowbrook. The use of these mentally retarded children as experimental subjects was a clear violation of their right to life and liberty.

Throughout most of the twentieth century, many "mildly retarded" persons have spent their entire lives institutionalized. Others have been involuntarily sterilized and denied educational opportunities. In cases where they have been considered "legally incompetent," they have not been able to marry, have children, live alone, or enter into contractual relationships without the consent of a guardian.

An Invisible, Silent Minority

Persons with mental, physical, and emotional disabilities have been an invisible, silent minority group in our society. These persons experience prejudice (pre-judgment): job discrimination and destructive misconceptions from able-bodied persons. Many people frequently exaggerate the true limitations of persons with disabilities. Some human beings are labeled as mentally retarded or emotionally limited when, in fact, they have no real disability.

Unlike other minority groups in the United States, such as African Americans and Hispanics, persons with disabilities do not form an obviously distinct group. What they do share, however, is frequent prejudice and discrimination from their peers, professionals, and even parents and other so-called "people who count" in our society. Also, some researchers have suggested that physical disabilities, vision and hearing impairment, and continual health impairments in children with disabilities occur more frequently among poor children than among rich children. Even among adults, studies reveal that disabilities are two or three times more common among the poor.

However, there are important differences between persons with disabilities and other minority groups. For one thing — unlike those who are born black or female — not all persons with disabilities are born as part of a minority; that is, they are not always born with their disabilities. Also, most persons with disabilities will not give birth to future generations of such persons.

The Disability Rights Movement

The disability rights movement is rooted in the right of all persons to life and liberty. While there were special schools for blind and deaf students in the 1860's, during the presidency of Abraham Lincoln, the struggle to protect the rights of persons with disabilities began in earnest only in the early 1950's. At that time, parents of children with disabilities began to meet to support one another and share their problems and experiences.

Persons with disabilities have often gone homeless. (Library of Congress)

People began to realize that if they worked together they had a better chance of helping their children and one another. Various advocacy groups sprang up, such as the Muscular Dystrophy Association of America, the National Federation of the Blind, the United Cerebral Palsy Associations, and the National Association for Retarded Children. These groups worked to raise money to support medical research on disabilities and recreation programs, and to find ways to help persons with disabilities who had to learn new ways to do things such as drive, talk, and write (rehabilitation).

In 1956, the law instituting Social Security Disability Insurance was passed by the government. That insurance provided money mostly for persons in their fifties with disabilities. Discrimination and prejudice against persons with disabilities was very strong. For example, seventeen states prohibited a person with epilepsy from marrying.

In 1957, an Oklahoma man, Hugh Deffner, received the Handicapped American of the Year Award of President Eisenhower's Committee on Employment of the Handicapped. The award ceremony had been scheduled to take place in the old U.S. Department of Labor Building. However, the only way inside the building was up a set of steps. Ironically, Mr. Deffner had to be carried up the steps of the building by two Marine guards on duty. It was the only way he could enter the building to participate in the event and receive his award.

In the early 1960's, African Americans were at the forefront of the Civil Rights movement. Dr. Martin Luther King, Jr., helped African Americans gain their right to vote. He spoke out against the economic differences between whites and blacks in America, and in favor of the ways in which nonviolent protest could bring about social change. The movement for "handicapped" rights began only after various laws were passed that gave African Americans and women certain civil rights.

African Americans were made to sit in the back of the bus before the early 1960's. However, persons with disabilities could not even get on the bus. Taking advantage of their First Amendment rights, they began to write letters to government officials, and to hold "wheel-ins," public demonstrations in which wheelchairs blocked entrances to government buildings. Many persons with disabilities and able-bodied persons worked hard to stop prejudice, discrimination, separation, and financial deprivation, which all contributed to a denial of the basic human and legal rights of persons with disabilities.

In the late 1960's and the early 1970's, the Vietnam War brought about an increased awareness of and struggle for the rights of persons with disabilities. Many veterans came home from the war with physical and mental impairments. These veterans began forming activist groups; they began to speak out against war and for the rights of persons with disabilities. They formed groups such as the Disabled American Veterans, the National Paraplegia Foundation, and the Paralyzed Veterans of America.

The Rehabilitation Act of 1973

The efforts of numerous disability rights activists and groups culminated in the passage of the Rehabilitation Act of 1973. This is sometimes referred to simply as the "Rehab Act," or P.L. (Public Law) 93-112. The Rehab Act is the basic federal law that contains funded programs and civil rights for persons with disabilities. It states, in Title V, that no otherwise qualified "handicapped" individual in the United States can, because of his or her disability, be "excluded from participation in, be denied benefits of, or be subjected to discrimination under any program or activity receiving federal financial assistance."

This act was patterned after the famous Title VI of the Civil Rights Act of 1964. The 1964 Civil Rights Act originally applied these words to discrimination based on race, color, or

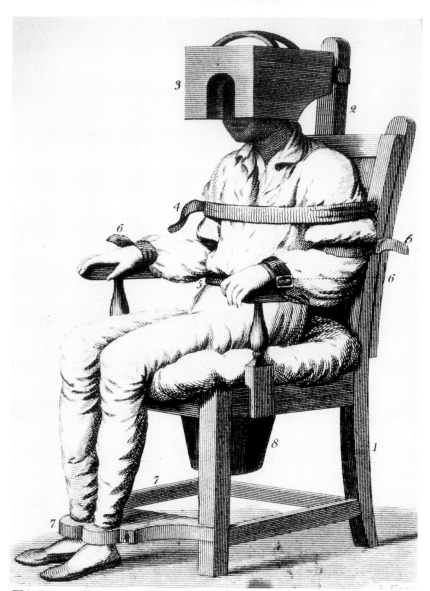

This "tranquillizing chair," invented by Benjamin Rush in 1811, was intended to calm those with mental illness. (National Library of Medicine)

national origin. Under the Rehab Act, the federal government states that it will not give financial aid to schools, hospitals, housing, transportation, and welfare programs that do not make their buildings accessible to persons with disabilities (Section 502). For many years after the act was passed, however, it was not enforced.

The Americans with Disabilities Act of 1990

An important victory of the disability rights movement is The Americans with Disabilities Act (ADA). This act became law on July 26, 1990, and went into effect in January, 1992. It was signed by President George Bush, who pledged that the United States would not accept, excuse, or tolerate discrimination in America. The ADA is a truly landmark civil rights bill. It has been called the "Emancipation Proclamation" for those with disabilities by its sponsors. The civil rights protections that it provides for persons with disabilities are similar to those guaranteed by other federal laws protecting the rights of other minority groups and women.

The ADA defines "disability" as (1) a physical or mental impairment that substantially limits an individual's life activities. The definition also applies to (2) any person having a record of an impairment or (3) the perception of having an impairment. Impaired sight and hearing, orthopedic muscular conditions such as cerebral palsy and muscular dystrophy, diseases such as cancer and epilepsy, and other disabilities (such as cosmetic disfigurement, emotional impairment, and low IQ) are also included in the congressional definition of disability.

The ADA also prohibits discrimination against individuals who have AIDS or the HIV virus, which leads to AIDS. The ADA does not, however, include illegal drug users, homosexuals, people with sexual disorders, and compulsive gamblers as persons with disabilities.

This landmark law has opened access to full participation in American life for persons with disabilities. The provisions of the ADA include employment opportunities, state and local government services, public accommodations, transportation, and the telephone system.

Implementing Disability Rights

Many Americans have worked hard to eliminate prejudice and discrimination based on race, color, religion, sex, and national origin. However, there is still much work to be done in order to implement the right to life and liberty for persons with disabilities. The courts cannot by themselves ensure the rights of persons with disabilities. Congress and state legislatures are also needed to enact rules and regulations that will guarantee these rights. It is the task of appropriate government agencies to see that disability rights are properly and truly enforced.

Persons with disabilities are not "disabled." (Bob Daemmrich/Uniphoto)

Chapter Two

Who Are Persons with Disabilities?

In the United States, more than forty-three million persons have disabilities. Roughly one-tenth of all children, one-fifth of all adults, and at least half of all able-bodied adults have a spouse, child, parent, or close friend with a disability. Disability can strike any person through an automobile accident, disease, environmental pollution, or old age. In fact, most people will experience some disability, at least temporarily, during their lifetimes.

Deaf and Hard-of-Hearing Persons

Deafness does not affect a person's intellectual capability or that person's ability to learn. A deaf person has a hearing impairment that is so severe that he or she cannot hear with or without the help of a hearing aid. An estimated sixteen million Americans have some degree of hearing impairment. More than two million Americans are totally deaf. The other fourteen million hearing-impaired Americans have less severe hearing losses, and they can often be helped to understand oral speech through the use of a hearing aid.

There are four types of hearing loss. *Conductive hearing losses* are caused by disease or obstructions in the outer or middle ear. Persons with a conductive hearing loss are usually able to use a hearing aid well. *Sensorineural hearing losses* result from damage to tiny hair cells or nerves of the inner ear. Persons with this type of hearing loss cannot use a hearing aid with any success. *Mixed hearing losses* result from problems in both the outer or middle earand the inner ear. Finally, a *central hearing loss* results from damage or impairment to nerves or cells of the person's central nervous system. In both mixed hearing loss and central hearing loss, hearing aids are helpful in some cases.

Deaf and Blind Persons

A deaf and blind person has both hearing and visual impairments. This combination causes severe communication,

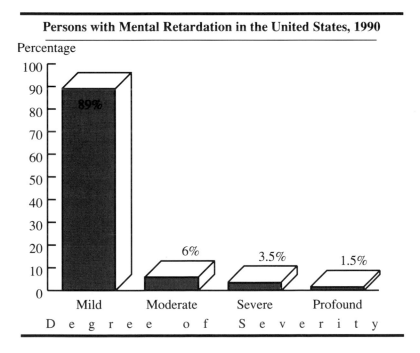

Persons with Mental Retardation in the United States, 1990

developmental, and educational problems. These persons cannot easily be accommodated in special education programs, which are usually designed solely for deaf persons or solely for blind persons. An estimated forty thousand people in the United States are "deaf-blind." About 70 percent became deaf first, then became blind later in life.

Persons with Mental Retardation

Mental retardation is a lifelong condition that results from a variety of causes, such as lack of food (malnutrition), heredity, chromosomal abnormalities, poor medical care before and after birth, or lack of environmental stimulation. In many cases, mental retardation can be prevented by proper health care before birth and access to good food both before birth and during infancy.

Mental retardation is neither a disease nor the same as mental illness or emotional disturbance. Mentally retarded persons have below-average intellectual capabilities. They have a hard time learning and applying what they learn. Mentally retarded persons are not all alike, because degrees of retardation vary from person to person. The vast majority of mentally retarded persons (89 percent) are only mildly retarded. Six percent are moderately retarded. Both mild and moderately retarded persons can care for themselves. Moderately retarded persons often need a highly supervised work setting. Severely retarded persons (about 3.5 percent) have impairments in motor development, speech and language, and often physical impairments as well. Profoundly retarded persons (about 1.5 percent) usually suffer physical impairments that make constant care necessary.

Between 6 and 7 million people in the United States are mentally retarded. Three percent of these persons live in institutions all their lives. The vast majority of persons with mental retardation have the capacity to learn, to develop, and to grow. They can become productive participants in society if able-bodied persons would only welcome their gifts and presence.

Persons with Learning Disabilities

Persons with learning disabilities differ in the degrees and combinations of their impairments. They might have a high, medium, or low intellectual capacity, but they usually have a hard time learning how to talk, how to read, or how to solve math problems at school. Children with learning disabilities often have a short attention span, a poor memory, and a difficult time following directions. Some persons cannot tell the difference between and among numbers, letters, and sounds — a condition known as *dyslexia*. For example, a person might read "saw" for the word "was." The former Olympic decathlon star Bruce Jenner has dyslexia, and so does the actor Tom Cruise.

Some children with learning disabilities are very active and restless; they have a condition called *hyperactivity*. Others are very slow and disorganized, and have difficulty relating with their family and friends. While the cause of many learning disabilities is unknown, there are many alternative ways of teaching children with such challenges.

Researchers are not sure how many children have learning disabilities. Some say that between 1 and 30 percent of children and adults have learning disabilities. The most common estimate is that 2 percent to 3 percent of school-aged children and youth have some form of learning disability. Some researchers suggest that as many as 10 percent of all Americans have some type of learning disability.

Many famous people have overcome learning disabilities to make major contributions to society. Thomas A. Edison was expelled from school in 1854. He had a learning disability that prevented him from doing well as a student. However, he went on to become one of the greatest American inventors, creating the electric light bulb.

Persons with Physical Disabilities

There are many different types of physical disabilities and special health problems. These can be the result of disease, birth defects, accidents, and exposure to poisonous chemicals in air, food, or water.

One of the most common physical disabilities is *arthritis*. Arthritis affects the joints in the body. Persons with arthritis suffer pain in some or all of their joints — toes, feet, knees, hips, fingers, jaw, back, and shoulder. Some 31 million persons have arthritis.

Meningitis, an infection that damages a young baby's brain, can lead to deafness or cause hydrocephalus (water or fluid on the brain) or other physical disabilities.

Cerebral palsy (CP) is caused by damage to different parts of the brain that control muscle movement. "Spastic," "athetoid," or "ataxic" cerebral palsy are different types of CP, describing different kinds of movements that persons with CP make as a result of damage to different areas of the brain. The damage usually occurs before, during, or right after birth, and is most frequently the result of a lack of oxygen at birth. Christy Brown was a man with cerebral palsy who wrote two books, *My Left Foot* (1954) and *Down All the Days* (1970), by typing with one toe. The United Cerebral Palsy Associations seeks solutions to various needs of persons with CP, such as finding a job and dealing with special health problems.

Epilepsy is a disorder of the nervous system that causes "seizures" (these are often wrongly called "fits" or "spells"). The brain cells of an epileptic person sometimes send too much electrical energy through the parts of the brain that control how people move, feel, or sense things. This "electrical overload" will cause a seizure to occur. A person

Conditions Reported as the Main Cause of Activity Limitation in the United States, 1983-1985

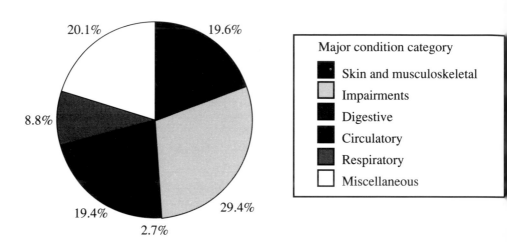

20.1% 19.6%

8.8%

19.4% 29.4%

2.7%

Major condition category

■ Skin and musculoskeletal

□ Impairments

■ Digestive

■ Circulatory

■ Respiratory

□ Miscellaneous

NOTE: Miscellaneous category includes conditions of the genitourinary, nervous, endocrine, metabloke, and blood-forming systems; cancer affecting sites other than these five categories; and mental illness.

SOURCE: M. P. LaPlante, *Data on Disability from the National Health Interview Survey, 1983-85.* Washington: National Institute on Disability and Rehabilitation Research, 1988. Reprinted by permission.

having a seizure cannot swallow his tongue, as is often believed.

A person with *multiple sclerosis* (MS) has many nerves that are scarred (*sclerosis* means "scar"). These scars of the nerves stop messages from the brain getting through to the person's muscles. As a result, the muscles get weak and eventually die. One out of three people with MS cannot walk. They need to use a wheelchair, brace, walker, or crutches to move around. Others cannot see because of their MS. Still others are tired all the time or feel like their arms and legs are very heavy. The

National Multiple Sclerosis Society in New York helps people learn more about the disease and helps those people who have it, and their families, to learn to live with the disease.

Muscular dystrophy (MD) is a disease that makes the body's muscles deteriorate over time. Children and adults with MD need to use a wheelchair, braces, or crutches to walk. About 30 out of every 100,000 children are born with MD. There is no cure for MD at the present time. Doctors treat patients with MD by means of surgery and exercises that help to make the diseased muscles stronger. The comedian Jerry Lewis has children with MD. He conducts a telethon every year to try to raise money to find a cure for MD.

Persons with Birth Defects

A birth defect is a part of the body that has not developed correctly before a baby is born. Many different kinds of disabilities result from birth defects. Some of the most common ones are cleft lip and cleft palate, spina bifida, and Down syndrome.

Cleft lip and cleft palate are relatively common birth defects (one out of every 750 births). "Cleft" means split, so a child born with cleft lip (sometimes called a harelip) and cleft palate has a split upper lip and upper roof of the mouth. With the help of a surgeon, orthodontist, dentist, and speech therapist, these conditions are most frequently corrected.

Spina bifida is an expression that comes from the Latin language and means "split spine." The baby's spinal cord sticks out through his or her backbone. This usually occurs when the mother is in the third or fourth week of pregnancy. Some children with spina bifida are mentally retarded, but the majority are just as intelligent as most other people. They may need to use a wheelchair to get around, but today they are able to work, marry, and have children.

Down syndrome is the most common known cause of mental retardation identified at birth. It occurs when the father's sperm cells and the mother's egg cells divide the wrong way. This faulty division results in one extra chromosome in the baby's body cells. Children with Down syndrome can learn many of the same things that other children can learn; it just takes them a longer time. Some graduate from high school. Others work in sheltered workshops, for example, stuffing envelopes, sorting hardware, or putting together parts to machinery. Some even have acting roles in television shows: Chris Burke, for example, stars in the television series *Life Goes On*.

Visually Impaired Persons

Blindness in an individual means that a person cannot see anything at all or has only the ability to see light. A person who is "legally blind" can see at a distance of twenty feet what a normally sighted person can see at a distance of two hundred feet. Blind persons learn and study by reading Braille (raised dots on paper or some other surface). They also use audio tools that do not require reading, such as cassette tapes or compact disks, to which they can listen.

Blindness and visual impairment increase as people grow older. In fact, blindness does not occur frequently in babies and children. Only about one out of every twenty-five hundred children is blind. Five million persons have visual impairments in the United States. About 8 percent of these persons are under the age of twenty, 37 percent are between the ages of twenty and sixty-four, and 55 percent are older than sixty-five years of age.

People should always speak directly to a blind person. Persons who guide a blind person, perhaps to help him or her cross a street, should let that person take one's arm above the elbow. Do not pet a blind person's guide dog when it is in a harness. Ask the blind person if he or she would like you to describe what you are seeing.

Emotionally Impaired Persons

More than 60 million Americans between the ages of eighteen and sixty-four will experience an emotional disability at some time in their life. Many technical terms are used to describe emotional disabilities, such as "behavior disorder," "psychological disorder," "schizophrenia," "mental illness," "neurosis," and "psychosis." A young person who is emotionally disturbed acts differently from most other children at a particular age.

The causes of emotional disturbance are not entirely clear, although one's family history or heredity, brain impairment,

These athletes happen to use wheelchairs. (Ken Regan/Special Olympics International)

diet, stress, and the use of drugs can all play a role in emotionally impairing a person. For many disturbances, medical and psychological assistance can help relieve a person's symptoms and achieve a cure.

Mobility-Impaired Persons

The major cause of paralysis in the United States results from automobile wrecks and swimming accidents. Persons who have muscle impairments of both their arms and legs are referred to as *quadriplegics*. Persons who have muscle impairment in their legs are referred to as *paraplegics*.

Some persons have to have a hand, arm, foot, or leg cut off (amputated) in order to stop a serious medical problem or infection. When that happens, they have to wear an artificial limb, called a *prosthesis*, in order to walk or hold things. Prosthetic devices cost a lot of money to buy and have fitted properly, and insurance often does not buy these devices unless they are implanted.

Franklin Delano Roosevelt was a president of the United States who needed a wheelchair. He ran the country as chief executive even though the disease polio impaired his mobility.

Chapter Three

The Right
to
Respect

The most important human right is the right to respect for one's dignity. The greatest barriers to human respect are negative attitudes, prejudice, and discrimination. Overcoming misconceptions or stereotypes about persons with disabilities is vital for the full implementation of their human rights.

"Handicapping" Persons with Disabilities

The origin of the term "handicap" is not entirely certain. Some suggest that the term began to be used in the nineteenth century during the Industrial Revolution. At that time, persons with physical or mental disabilities were ostracized. They often had to beg for food and money with their "cap in hand." Eventually they came to be called "handy-cappers."

In the past, a disability or "handicap" was wrongly equated with sickness and weakness. Consequently, the term "handicap" is not a satisfactory term, even if it is found in many government laws and documents. The truth is that persons without disabilities are the ones that often handicap persons with disabilities through negative attitudes and other types of barriers.

In the past, societal attitudes and government laws concerning persons with disabilities were commonly expressed in negative terms. For example, persons with emotional disturbance were labeled "insane" and put in an "asylum." Persons with physical disabilities were spoken of as "cripples" or "spastics." These are insulting and negative labels that have no place in society today. Persons in a wheelchair have been labeled as "confined" or "wheel-chair-bound." The preferred term to use is "mobility-impaired." A wheelchair or crutches used by a person become very much a part of that person's "body."

Speaking About Disabilities: Do's and Don'ts

Do Say	Don't Say
Persons with disabilities	Handicapped, disabled
Down syndrome	Mongolism
Cleft lip	Harelip
Mobility-impaired	Crippled, spastic, retarded
Deaf and hearing impaired	Deaf and dumb
Seizure	Fit, spell
Speech-impaired	Mute, dumb, stutterer
Mentally impaired	Idiot, moron, deficient
Emotionally impaired	Crazy, mental case
Able-bodied person	Normal
Temporarily able-bodied	Normal

While there is a real physical difference between persons with disabilities and "able-bodied" persons, this difference has nothing to do with a person's worth. What it means to others and to oneself to have a disability is primarily a social reality. Labeling people is never acceptable. Both persons with disabilities and those without disabilities must be sensitive to each other *as persons*, created with human dignity.

Stereotyping Persons with Disabilities

It is necessary to change false stereotypes if the right to respect is to be fully recognized. The word "stereotype" comes from two Greek words and literally means a "solid type." A stereotype of persons with disabilities means that a particular type of false image or idea has become solid, or fixed, in people's minds. False stereotypes of persons with disabilities have resulted from their historical separation from the mainstream of society.

Numerous false stereotypes about persons with disabilities exist. The most common false stereotype is that disability equals inability. Just because a person uses a wheelchair or is hearing-impaired or vision-impaired does not mean that he or she need be excluded from working and enjoying life. A person with a physical or mobility impairment should not be prejudged as having a mental inability or deficiency. Many persons with disabilities simply view their impairment or disability as an inconvenience. The National Organization on Disability in Washington, D.C., promotes full participation of America's 43 million persons with disabilities. To stress that a disability is not the same thing as inability, they print the word "disability" on their letterhead like this:

DISABILITY

Here are some of the many other false beliefs about persons with disabilities:

MYTH: Persons with disabilities cannot speak for themselves. It is necessary to ask an able-bodied person who is with a deaf or blind person what the deaf or blind person wants.
FACT: This image stems from an earlier, paternalistic attitude that prevailed when society believed it was up to "normal" persons to pity and care for persons with disabilities.

MYTH: All persons with disabilities are hearing-impaired.

FACT: Hearing-impaired persons may constitute a large percentage of persons with disabilities, but not all persons with disabilities are hearing-impaired. Able-bodied persons sometimes tend to shout at those with any kind of impairment — not just those with hearing loss — because they mistakenly (or even unconsciously) think that all physical impairments limit one's capacity to hear.

MYTH: Those with hearing impairments can automatically read lips.

FACT: Not all persons with hearing impairments can read lips. Moreover, statistics suggest that, at the very best, a person who reads lips can understand 60 to 70 percent of the words spoken. Often the percentage is less than 50 percent. In other words, the use of a hearing aid and the partial ability to lip-read usually do not restore perfect hearing.

MYTH: All blind persons can read Braille.

FACT: At most, 15 percent of persons with vision impairment read Braille.

MYTH: There is no real need for parking spaces designated for persons with disabilities.

FACT: As a result of this attitude, some able-bodied people will use these conveniently located parking spaces, even though doing so is illegal. The fact is that people with physical or mobility impairments often suffer because of these selfish persons.

MYTH: All persons with learning disabilities have the same problem.

FACT: Learning disabilities are not all alike. Each person with a learning disability is different, and the degree of that disability is different. The right to respect requires that each person be treated as a unique individual.

MYTH: Mental retardation is contagious, like a cold virus.
FACT: People who believe this myth tend to shun or fear mentally retarded persons, as though they might "catch" their "disease." Others believe that mentally retarded persons are dangerous — that they might do something violent or crazy at any moment. There is no evidence whatsoever to suggest that mentally retarded persons are dangerous, and they are certainly not "contagious."

MYTH: All persons in wheelchairs must stay in their chairs.
FACT: In reality, many persons who use a wheelchair may use it only some of the time. They can often transfer themselves to a couch or another chair.

MYTH: Buildings that have rampways are accessible to all persons with disabilities.
FACT: A building that has a ramp is *not* necessarily "accessible." A building is truly accessible if and only if a person with a disability can both enter and use the building once inside.

MYTH: Persons with disabilities are unhappy.
FACT: Ron Judkins, a mobility-impaired person, has an answer to this myth. When able-bodied persons ask him how he can have such a good attitude, even though he has a disability, he asks in response: "How can so many able-bodied persons be so *un*happy?" Persons with disabilities have the same range of emotions and feelings as everyone else.

MYTH: People without disabilities assume that people who have certain disabilities must also have a given set of other limitations.
FACT: Certain disabilities do create limitations. However, these limitations vary from person to person, and they are based on a given individual's ability to adapt one's disability to a desired lifestyle.

MYTH: People without disabilities commonly think that persons who have disabilities are asexual beings.
FACT: This is misguided thinking, since even persons with the most severe disabilities have sexual urges. Many persons do not acknowledge or cannot accept this fact.

Stereotyping Persons Without Disabilities

Much has been written about the negative attitudes that able-bodied persons have toward persons with disabilities. These societal attitudes hinder respect for the human dignity of able-bodied persons. The National Easter Seal Society (NESS) is one of many organizations that works to eliminate negative stereotypes and prejudice against persons with disabilities. NESS has also identified ten "myths" and "facts" about persons *without* disabilities.

MYTH: The first myth is that people without disabilities do not want to meet or be around persons who have disabilities.
FACT: The fact is that many able-bodied persons often do not have any experience with persons with disabilities and therefore they are uncomfortable. NESS recommends that persons with disabilities reach out and introduce themselves to their able-bodied peers. This will help put them at ease and will break down personal barriers and negative attitudes.

MYTH: When a person has a disability, people offer help only out of pity.
FACT: An offer of help may simply be a proper act of courtesy. Those with disabilities should accept or decline an offer of assistance in a polite manner, and leave all avenues of communication open.

MYTH: People who offer help to persons with disabilities usually know how to give the help that is needed.
FACT: Good intentions are not the same thing as skill. If a person with a disability accepts assistance, he or she should give specific instructions on what kind of help would be useful and how such help should be provided.

MYTH: People always offer assistance when they see someone who might need it.
FACT: Many people hesitate to get involved. Many fear the unknown, or have had a previous bad experience when they have tried to help someone. More significant is that many people simply have an apathetic attitude. If one asks for help, one will probably receive the needed assistance.

MYTH: Persons without disabilities are obligated to provide a wide range of special services and treatment for people who have disabilities.
FACT: Certain accommodations have a legal and moral basis. However, people without disabilities are not obligated to right all the wrongs that people with disabilities may encounter as they go through life.

MYTH: Most people know little about the lifestyles of their neighbors who have disabilities, and they really do not want to know more.

FACT: Just because someone does not know about something does not mean that that person does not care. Most people simply do not think about disability-related rights and needs.

MYTH: It is acceptable to label people without disabilities as "A.B.'s" (able-bodied), "T.A.B.'s" (temporarily able-bodied), or "normals."
FACT: Labeling people is never acceptable. "Able-bodied" and "temporarily able-bodied" are relative terms, and the use of the term "normal" is acceptable only when it is applied to statistical norms and averages.

MYTH: Just because people without disabilities can never truly experience the full ramifications of disability-related problems, they should never represent people who have disabilities on boards or in organizations concerned with disability issues and rights.
FACT: This kind of exclusion is a form of reverse discrimination. Involvement by people without disabilities in disability activities, awareness, and rights issues can enlighten and enhance a group's collective intelligence and ability.

Changing Public Attitudes

The very first national survey of public attitudes toward people with disabilities was commissioned by the National Organization on Disability in 1991. The poll was conducted by Louis Harris and Associates, and it asked:

- What contact have Americans had with people with disabilities?
- What are Americans' feelings toward people with disabilities?

- Do Americans perceive discrimination against persons with disabilities?
- How do Americans feel about the expanded participation of people with disabilities in the mainstream of American life?
- What do Americans know about the Americans with Disabilities Act (ADA)?

A choir of deaf children: Singing is not limited to those who can hear. (Bob Daemmrich/ Uniphoto)

The survey showed that almost half of the American public know people with disabilities as friends, relatives, neighbors, or co-workers. One-third of Americans have a close friend or relative who has a disability. Better-educated and younger Americans know the most about persons with disabilities.

Americans' feelings toward persons with disabilities varies from awkwardness to embarrassment to pity to admiration. With respect to the fuller participation of persons with disabilities in American society, the survey revealed that 92 percent believe that society will benefit economically from the participation of persons with disabilities. Fully 98 percent believe that everyone, including persons with disabilities, should have an equal opportunity to participate in American society. Most important, 78 percent of those polled see people with disabilities as an "underused potential" in the American workplace.

Two out of every three adults believe that people with disabilities are discriminated against in employment. A little less than 47 percent see discrimination in their access to public transportation and in equal pay for equal work. Nearly all Americans, 96 percent, support making restaurants, stores, theaters, and hotels accessible. Almost as many, 93 percent, support making public transportation accessible. Of those surveyed, 89 percent believe that the ADA will be worth the unspecified costs of implementing it.

Movies and television programs have helped change public attitudes toward persons with disabilities. The most important films cited in the Harris poll were *Rain Man* (1988), *Children of a Lesser God* (1986), *Born on the Fourth of July* (1989), and *My Left Foot* (1989). The most important television series cited were *L.A. Law* and *Life Goes On*.

Chapter Four

The Right
to
Access

The right to access means the right of persons with disabilities to approach, enter, and use a facility or transportation vehicles in a safe and convenient manner. In 1969, Rehabilitation International — an organization with branches in eighty-three countries which conducts programs for the rehabilitation of persons with physical and mental disabilities — presented a wheelchair as a symbol of access. This symbol has been adopted as a means of indicating accessibility to buildings, parking areas, and transportation vehicles. Some persons have criticized this symbol as too specific and not symbolic of other disabilities. Others have seen it as a negative rather than a positive symbol. Overall, however, the symbol of the wheelchair has served a useful purpose. When the right of persons with disabilities to access is fully realized, there will be no need for the wheelchair symbol; instead, a symbol would be needed only if access were impossible.

Barriers to Access

Until recently, architects and engineers have designed buildings and facilities in America to meet the needs of able-bodied, right-handed adults. Virtually every road, building,

The international access symbol. (Reprinted by permission of Rehabilitation International)

curb, stair, escalator, doorway, and aisle have been built in a way that prevents persons with disabilities from reaching their destination. Buildings have been constructed with stairs and no rampways or elevators, inaccessible to persons in wheelchairs; with fire alarms that cannot be heard by deaf persons; and with no tactile marks to allow blind persons to find their way through hallways.

Such barriers affect all aspects of the lives of persons with disabilities. These barriers determine which schools one may attend, where one can find work, which transportation facilities one may use, and which recreational facilities one might enjoy. For example, it is difficult, if not impossible, to make a new friend when one cannot enter through the door of that person's house or apartment. Doors must be at least thirty inches wide if a wheelchair is to pass through. However, almost all doors in the United States are narrower than twenty-four inches. Furthermore, a person with limited twisting motion in the wrist cannot open most doors. Doors designed with handles that require only downward pressure instead of a twisting motion are accessible to most persons with physical impairments.

A Start Toward Access

In 1959, the President's Committee on Employment of the Handicapped, the (then called) National Easter Seal Society for Crippled Children and Adults, and other private and public disability rights groups began an effort to eliminate architectural barriers. Their work led to the publication of a document, *Specifications for Making Buildings and Facilities Accessible to, and Usable by, the Physically Handicapped*, published in 1961 by the American National Standards Institute (ANSI). The ANSI document was the first to raise awareness of access problems. It outlined the basic requirements for constructing government buildings that would be accessible to persons with disabilities. The standards set forth in the document included (1) at least one ground-level entrance to a

Signs on telephone booths showing the international access symbol let those with disabilities know that they can use the facility. (American Association for the Advancement of Science)

building; (2) the use of ramps in at least one location; (3) doorways thirty-two inches wide or wider; (4) rest rooms that can accommodate wheelchairs; (5) access to elevators; and (6) safe parking for persons with disabilities. The ANSI document has remained an important accessibility tool through the years.

The Architectural Barriers Act

The Architectural Barriers Act (ABA), P.L. 90-480, was passed by Congress in 1968. The act states that any building "constructed or leased in whole or in part with federal funds must be accessible to and usable by the physically handicapped." The ABA was not very effective because it pertained only to public buildings. The act excluded military buildings and privately constructed housing, and it was never really enforced.

Violations of the ABA

Despite the passage of the ABA, violations of the right to access have been commonplace. In 1972, a mobility-impaired attorney from Cleveland, Ohio, filed a class-action lawsuit against the county of Cuyahoga in Ohio (*Friedman v. County of Cuyahoga*). He was unable to roll his wheelchair up two flights of steep stairs to enter the court house because there were no rampways that allowed his wheelchair to move into the building. He argued that the building's lack of access violated his constitutional right to petition — a right guaranteed by the First Amendment. He also argued that the building's barriers violated his right to equal protection, the right to freedom of movement, and the right to equal opportunity guaranteed in the Fourteenth Amendment. The outcome was a decree in which the county promised to make all county-owned buildings accessible.

In 1974, another lawsuit was filed on behalf of persons with mobility impairment who were unable to vote because they

"THANKS FOR INVITING ME
TO SPEAK ON THE PROBLEMS
OF WHEELCHAIR USERS."

SOURCE: Copyright 1991, Para-
lyzed Veterans of America.
Reprinted by permission of
Paraplegia News.

could not enter polling places. In the case of *Seph et al.* v.
Council of the City of Los Angeles et al., the person who filed
the lawsuit (plaintiff) argued that this lack of access violated
the constitutional right to vote. The judge suggested that
persons with disabilities use the absentee ballot instead. The
plaintiff argued that forcing persons with disabilities to use an
absentee ballot segregates and discourages them in the voting
process.

In 1984, the Voting Accessibility for the Elderly and
Handicapped Act became law. This act requires that all polling
places for general elections (general, primary, and special) be
accessible to temporarily or permanently physically
handicapped voters. Moreover, each state is required to have a
reasonable number of polling places that are accessible to
persons with disabilities.

The Rehabilitation Act of 1973

Because the ABA was not being enforced properly,
Congress passed the influential Rehabilitation Act of 1973 (P.L.

93-112). Among other things, the "Rehab Act" authorized, under Section 502, the creation of the Architectural and Transportation Barriers Compliance Board (ATBCB) in order to enforce the provisions of the ABA. Most persons in the disability rights movement believe that the ATBCB does not have enough money to work effectively. The board has the authority to withhold funds from any building or facility that does not meet the board's standards. The board has indeed resolved numerous complaints through the years. It has also held public hearings to help Americans understand the barriers it seeks to remove.

Access to "Public Accommodations"

Title III of the Americans with Disabilities Act (1990) is called "Public Accommodations." An "accommodation" is a change in a program or a job in order to make it accessible to persons with disabilities. Title III prohibits discrimination against persons with disabilities in the full and equal enjoyment of the goods, services, facilities, privileges, advantages, or accommodations of any place of public accommodation.

Places of public accommodation include places of lodging, such as inns, hotels, and motels (except in those cases where the owner resides and rents out fewer than five rooms); establishments that serve food or drink; places of entertainment; gathering places, such as auditoriums and city convention centers; retail sales establishments, such as bakeries, grocery stores, and clothing stores; service establishments, such as laundromats, banks, and doctors' and lawyers' offices; public transportation terminals; cultural facilities, such as museums, libraries, and art galleries; parks and zoos; places of education; social service centers, including day care centers and food banks; and places of exercise or health recreation, such as golf courses, health spas, and bowling alleys. All new facilities must be readily accessible and usable by persons with disabilities. The exceptions are buildings that are no more than three stories high or less than three thousand square feet.

Owners or operators of public accommodations are not allowed to discriminate against persons with disabilities. They must make "reasonable accommodation" to change structures that provide access to, and use of, public accommodations for persons with disabilities. An individual with a disability has the right to be given an equal opportunity to obtain services or goods. Under Title III, for example, a restaurant does not have to provide Braille menus for blind customers. However, the restaurant must have an employee read the menu aloud if necessary.

Barriers to Transportation

In today's world, transportation requires cars, trains, subways, buses, airplanes, and even facilities such as stations and overpasses. Access to various types of transportation is crucial if persons with disabilities are to realize their full human rights. A person with a disability cannot obtain food, medical supplies and treatment, cannot make friends, and cannot enjoy recreational, cultural, or sporting events if he or she cannot get to the locations where these events and people are found.

For many persons with disabilities, driving a car is not a major problem. Hand controls make it possible for a person who cannot use his or her legs to drive. Special turn-signal devices and lifts make roads and highways accessible for many physically impaired persons. Obtaining a driver's license is sometimes a legal problem. Each state has the authority to regulate who is able to drive. Some states require proof of a six-month or one-year seizure-free period for persons with epilepsy. The Epilepsy Foundation of America provides

Buses in Washington, D.C., can be boarded by those in wheelchairs. (Washington Metropolitan Area Transit Authority)

additional information on state-by-state requirements concerning driving and epilepsy.

Many buses, subways, trains, planes, and transportation terminals still remain inaccessible to most persons with severe disabilities. Access to subway stations is often limited by curbs and other physical barriers. In fact, there is no city in the United States or Canada where transportation is as accessible to persons with disabilities as it is to able-bodied persons.

The Washington Metro case was one of the first known instances in American history in which a public facility was delayed because of its lack of access to persons with disabilities. In 1973, the decision in the court case *Washington Urban League, Inc. et al.* v. *Washington Metropolitan Area Transit Authority, Inc.* resulted in a prohibition that stopped the new Metro system from operating until all of its facilities were made accessible.

In 1973, the Federal-Aid Highway Act (P.L. 93-87) specified that various highway projects be accessible. This act included the requirement that all streets built with federal funds have their curbs cut out or ramps installed at intersections.

The Air Carriers Access Act (ACAA) was passed by Congress in 1986. A subsection states that no air carrier may discriminate in providing air transportation to any otherwise qualified "handicapped" individual because of that person's "handicap."

Paratransit Systems

Paratransit systems are vans that take persons with disabilities door to door or provide other transportation alternatives such as taxicab fare reductions. While these services are great improvements over the past, they are still separate from the mainstream means of transportation. And separate facilities mean less than equal transportation access. In fact, surveys suggest that a high percentage of paratransit systems are still unable to serve the transportation needs of persons with disabilities.

Transportation and the ADA

The Americans with Disabilities Act of 1990 addressed some key issues concerning the right to accessible transportation. The ADA required that qualified individuals with disabilities not be denied insurance based on their disability alone. It also required that all new buses bought by public transit authorities be accessible. Paratransit services, where not an enormous financial burden, must be provided for persons with disabilities who cannot use the regular bus system. Finally, the ADA requires that all train facilities be accessible.

Human beings create the environment in which they live, and they can thus remove obstacles that stand in the way of the right to access. Blind persons may not be able to read printed signs or directions, but they can understand raised letters. Deaf persons may not be able to hear spoken announcements or fire alarms, but printed instructions and lights in a building make facilities more accessible. Elevator buttons do not have to be located out of the reach of people in wheelchairs. Ramps that enable persons to get around using stairs do not have to be sloped so steeply as to be dangerous. Buses and paratransit systems can be designed to be boarded by anyone. It is of great value to society to have barrier-free facilities and transportation systems. Full access makes persons with disabilities more independent and aids in their opportunities for employment. Increased independence and access far outweighs the costs of making facilities and transportation systems accessible.

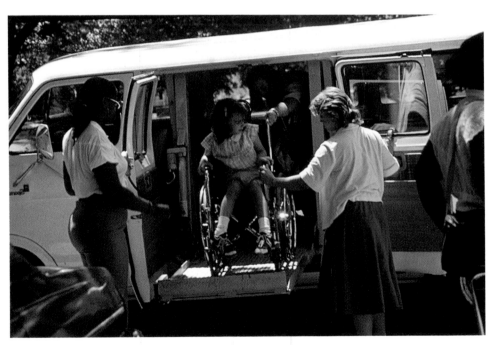

Special vans with lifts accommodate those in wheelchairs. (American Association for the Advancement of Science)

Chapter Five

The Right
to
Housing

One of the long-cherished dreams of American life is the opportunity to live in a satisfactory, convenient, and affordable home. To own one's own home is also a dream of persons with disabilities, but it is even more of a necessity, since most apartment buildings are inaccessible. Because access barriers are everywhere in the environment, persons with disabilities desire housing in which they are in control — where there are no constraints and where they can feel safe and secure.

Barriers to Housing

The historical reality for most persons with disabilities has been physical and psychological separation in state institutions. They have been forced to live, often against their will, in the homes of other persons, in an institution, or in dilapidated apartment buildings. It is virtually impossible to find accessible private housing. Builders of private homes are under no legal constraints to build accessible dwellings. One man with a mobility impairment since 1944 lived in nine different cities and six different states during a period of well over thirty years. He was unable to find an accessible home or apartment until the mid-1970's.

Historical developments in housing alternatives have expanded to include group homes, hostels, halfway houses, foster homes, mobile homes, sheltered living arrangements, group apartments, and independent living centers. Most persons with disabilities seek housing within the mainstream of the community, not apart from it.

Special elevators allow access to upper floors. (American Association for the Advancement of Science)

It is difficult to separate housing problems for persons with disabilities from the general housing situation and economy of society. Poverty, discrimination, prejudice, and lack of affordable housing affect many persons. While the United States is a wealthy country with a relatively small population compared to some other countries in the world, approximately every two in five families in the United States is in urgent need of housing. The right to housing for persons with disabilities and the elderly is even more difficult to secure and implement.

Adaptations and Accessibility

Accessible entrance to a home is crucial. The average wheelchair is about two feet and one inch in width. Motorized wheelchairs are often two and one-half feet wide. However, doors in the United States are usually twenty-four inches wide.

Doorways, walkways, and approaches to doors need to be three feet wide, as do ramps. Rampways should be gentle rather than steep in slope. Because climbing long ramps in a wheelchair is tiring, they should be no more than thirty feet long. They should also have guardrails in order to prevent a wheelchair from rolling off.

Kitchen adaptations for those with disabilities should include vertical drawers that rest on the floor, lowered sinks or counters, and push-button turntables for plates, cutlery, and other kitchen utensils. Bathrooms are frequently the most

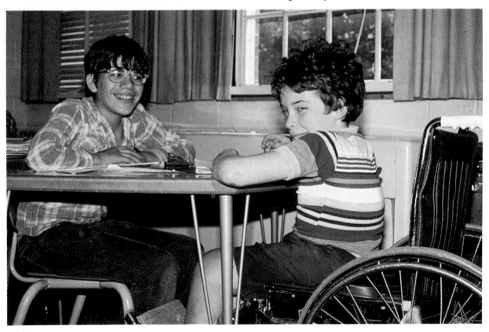

Furniture is not always built with the needs of those with disabilities in mind. (American Association for the Advancement of Science)

inaccessible room in an apartment or house. Sinks and toilets, medicine chests, mirrors, and wall electrical outlets need to be within reach.

The Superintendent of Documents at the Government Printing Office in Washington, D.C., provides literature related to adaptations and types of housing for persons with physical disabilities.

Federal Housing Legislation

The most important housing law enacted in the 1940's was the Housing Act of 1949 (P.L. 81-171). This act made persons with disabilities eligible for inclusion in projects sponsored by the Department of Housing and Urban Development (HUD). Between 1941 and 1964, virtually no housing units were built for persons with disabilities. However, during the 1960's, new housing programs were begun. Persons with disabilities began to be recognized as a group that had a right to special services. The 1965 Housing and Urban Development Act (P.L. 89-117) included persons with disabilities and the elderly as beneficiaries of rent subsidy. Between 1964 and 1975, one thousand dwelling units were designed and constructed for persons with disabilities under the auspices of HUD.

The single most important federal housing legislation has been the Housing and Community Development Act of 1974 (P.L. 93-383). Under this act, the federal government provided financial subsidies for alternative living arrangements for persons with disabilities. These arrangements included group homes and congregate housing in which a central kitchen and dining facilities are shared. The act also provided rent subsidies and other money for projects designed to remove access barriers to make facilities and means of transportation accessible.

The Rehabilitation, Comprehensive Services, and Developmental Disabilities Amendments of 1978 (P.L.

95-602), signed by President Jimmy Carter, authorized a four-part program for "independent living" (IL). First, an IL services program was established, to be administered by the United States' eighty-four state vocational rehabilitation agencies, coordinating a broad program of IL rehabilitation services. Second, the law stated that government funds would be distributed through these eighty-four agencies directly to IL centers around the country. Third, the amendments established an IL program for older blind persons. Finally, they provided a protection and advocacy program to safeguard the rights of persons with severe disabilities.

The Independent Living Movement

The Independent Living (IL) Movement is the key to the door to housing rights for persons with disabilities. The IL movement is concerned with creative ways of living. Its primary focus has been on persons with severe disabilities, particularly persons with spinal cord injuries, muscular dystrophy, cerebral palsy, multiple sclerosis, and post-polio disablement. The IL movement has concentrated its energies on older adolescents and younger working adults. IL programs are community-based, and thus they depend on the people and resources within the community for their success.

The IL movement may be traced to efforts by persons with disabilities to seek their right to participate in a world of able-bodied persons, and by rehabilitation professionals who were concerned with the vocational goals of persons with disabilities. In 1962, four students with severe disabilities at the University of Illinois at Champaign-Urbana sought a transfer from a nursing home to an accessible home near campus; many trace the origin of IL to this event. In the early 1970's, a Center for Independent Living was established in Berkeley, California, by Judy Heumann and Ed Roberts. The center provides a range of services such as peer counseling, legal assistance, van transportation, training in independent living skills, attendant care or nursing assistance, health-care tips, housing referrals, and wheelchair repair. The Boston Center for Independent Living began in 1974. The Boston Center emphasizes short-term housing arrangements after release from hospital services.

A growing number of bathroom facilities are designed to accommodate those in wheelchairs. (American Association for the Advancement of Science)

The Housing and Community Development Act of 1974 directly sponsored eight projects to demonstrate and study different models of independent living for persons with severe disabilities. These were located in Los Angeles, Toledo, Seattle, Omaha, Fall River, Fargo, Columbus, and Houston. During this same period, the Texas Institute for Rehabilitation and Research in Houston was on the cutting edge of independent living programs. Four innovative programs are called Independent Lifestyles, Spring Tree, Free Lives, and Cooperative Living. Independent Lifestyles, for example, provides housing and attendant or nursing services for persons with severe disabilities. Each resident is responsible for his or her own apartment and meal preparation. A staff of attendants help with meal preparation. The community also owns a van and employs a driver on a full-time basis. Most of the residents hold full-time jobs.

Raised dots, or Braille, allow blind persons using this elevator to get to the right floor. (Frank Siteman/Uniphoto)

Self-Determination and Independence

Independent living means allowing persons with disabilities to live as they choose in their communities. IL provides persons with severe disabilities a space for self-determination and independence. IL also involves a number of challenges. A person with a disability who chooses independent living must exchange the safety of custodial care for the risk and effort involved in making decisions and taking actions that will shape his or her life. IL means finding and maintaining one's own support services.

More than one-half million persons with severe disabilities are living comparatively independent lives as a result of the services provided by independent living programs throughout U.S. and Canadian cities.

Chapter Six

The Right to Education

One-half or more children and youth with disabilities in North America are receiving an inappropriate education. Poor education restricts the right of persons with disabilities to education at levels beyond the middle school and high school years. This restriction, in turn, affects their chance for a good job that will earn a decent living.

Special Education

The term "special education" refers to the educational services schools offer for children with exceptional physical, emotional, intellectual, or perceptual limitations. Researchers estimate that nine million children and youths aged three to twenty-one require special education services. Once a child is labeled "disabled" and in need of special education, he or she has only a ten percent chance of returning to a regular classroom.

Special education for children with disabilities is a recent phenomenon. Some special schools were established in the 1890's, but most of these were residential facilities and asylums for mentally retarded persons or institutions for the deaf. Special education has its real roots in the 1930's. At that time, nearly every large American city had some type of special education service for children with disabilities. These services included individual classrooms for children with mental retardation or hearing impairment, special classes for those with physical disabilities, and "remedial" classes in speech improvement.

Under President Roosevelt, Crippled Children's Services (CCS) was established for children with disabilities. Its purpose was, and is, to provide specialized medical care and rehabilitation for children with disabilities whose families are unable to pay for the total cost of expensive medical bills. A large portion of public medical treatment and care is still provided through CCS, though the name is now inappropriate. Services are found in every state and the District of Columbia, as well as in American Samoa, Guam, the Northern Mariana Islands, Puerto Rico, the Trust Territory, and the Virgin Islands.

In the mid-1960's, parents of children with disabilities became involved with special education, because they realized that more could be done to help their children achieve their full potential. Parents began to demand alternatives to placing their children in institutions. They wanted educational opportunities for their children that were equal to those of able-bodied persons. In 1965, the Elementary and Secondary Education Act was passed. Title I of that act included "handicapped" children in its provisions. The Education of the Handicapped Act of 1969 (P.L. 91-230), expanded the 1965 act. Section 504 of the 1973 Rehabilitation Act mandated that public schools provide academic educational services, counseling, extracurricular activities, physical education, health, and transportation services necessary for students with disabilities to realize their right to equal opportunity education.

The Developmental Disabilities Assistance and Bill of Rights Act, and the Developmental Disabilities, Rehabilitation,

"Crippled" children in a 1930's schoolroom. (National Archives)

and Comprehensive Services Amendments of 1978 (P.L. 95-602) discarded earlier developmental definitions of disabilities to include two hundred different types. The general purpose of this federal law was to increase the availability of services to persons with developmental disabilities, including educational services. Since 1978, a developmental disability has been defined as any severe, chronic (or permanent) disability resulting from a mental or physical impairment. The disability must pose a long-term barrier in three or more areas, such as communication, self-care, learning, mobility, self-direction, independent living, or economic self-sufficiency. The law seeks to improve the availability, quality, and coordination of developmental disabilities services. The law encourages deinstitutionalization and promotes individualized habilitation, including individualized education programs.

The PARC and Mills Cases

Several lawsuits filed in the early 1970's led to the right of persons with disabilities to free, public education. In 1971, the Pennsylvania Association for Retarded Children (PARC) argued that mentally retarded children could learn if their right to an appropriate education were recognized. In *PARC* v. *Commonwealth of Pennsylvania*, the federal court agreed for the first time that mentally retarded children had a right to equal access to public education. Part of the PARC decision was the ruling that a school could not assign a child with a disability to a special education class without first informing the child's parents. Parents could in turn challenge such a decision if they did not agree with the ruling. The court also stated that it was better to place retarded children in a regular

Children learning in an orthopedic school. (Jeffry W. Myers/Uniphoto)

public school class ("the least restrictive environment") than in a special education public school class.

In 1972, in *Mills* v. *Board of Education of District of Columbia*, the court argued that all individuals with any kind of emotional or physical disability have a right to equal access to public education. This case went beyond the PARC case by extending the right to public education to all persons with disabilities. The court also argued that "insufficient funds" was no excuse for denying persons with disabilities equal access to education.

The PARC and Mills decisions are important because they affirmed five important principles. First, education is a human right and not simply a privilege for persons with disabilities. Second, schools must legally offer equal educational opportunities. Third, children with disabilities must be placed in the least restrictive educational environment as possible. Fourth, a child with a disability is entitled to an education that meets his or her particular needs, and not just some needs. Finally, parents of children with disabilities are entitled to have their educational wishes known (procedural due process).

The Education for All Handicapped Children Act

The 1975 Education for All Handicapped Children Act (EAHCA), P.L. 94-142, is the most significant legislation concerning the right to education. The primary goal of the act is to implement the right to education of every child with a disability. The Act states that a free appropriate public education is to be made available for all children with disabilities from three to twenty-one years of age. The law limits the number of children with disabilities to twelve percent of the entire school-age population between the ages of five and seventeen.

In order for states to receive federal financial grants under the EAHCA they must meet six conditions.

(1) They must locate, identify, and evaluate every child with a disability within their jurisdiction.

(2) They must conduct evaluations of children with disabilities in a nondiscriminatory manner.

(3) States must place children in the least restrictive environment consistent with their special needs.

(4) States must see to it that the parents or guardians of children with disabilities are given their due process rights, including a fair hearing on any matter concerning their child's education.

(5) States must provide inservice training for special educators and support persons.

(6) States must pay for educational services and guarantee all rights to children with disabilities in private facilities or schools also.

By 1981, just over 8.5 percent of the school-age population was receiving special education services under EAHCA. In 1990, the EAHCA was renamed the Individuals with Disabilities Education Act (IDEA), P.L. 101-476. The act had the effect of expanding government assistance to include "social rehabilitation." Social rehabilitation is assistance to include improving adjustment to life in the community and relationships with other persons.

Individualized Education Programs

Individualized education programs (IEP) came into existence by law with the passage of the EAHCA. The EAHCA mandated that special education programs require planning for children with disabilities based on the individual child's needs. A written IEP requires analysis of a child's educational ability, a statement of annual goals, short-term objectives for achieving the identified goals, and special education and related services.

Mainstreaming

Mainstreaming has been a controversial subject in the establishment of a right to education for persons with disabilities. The philosophy behind mainstreaming is that a person has the greatest chance of achieving his or her educational autonomy and independence by being placed in as

Working hard in school is important for all students, with or without a wheelchair. (American Association for the Advancement of Science)

normal, or least restrictive, an environment as possible. Public schools have been designed to educate the average "normal" child. Children with disabilities are often put in special education programs that segregate them by their disabilities. The ideal is that they be segregated according to their abilities and interests. Just because two children have the same disabilities, it does not mean that they have the same abilities.

Once a person is labeled "disabled," the disability tends to be perceived and expected by teachers and other educators over time. A child who is labeled "mildly mentally retarded," for example, will often receive less, or less challenging, instruction than an average student, because the teacher expects the child to be unable to benefit from instruction. Because less is expected from the student labeled mildly retarded, that child learns less. The label, therefore, reinforces the disability.

Some educators and public officials complain that implementing the right to education of persons with disabilities is too costly. It is true that accommodations for mainstreaming persons with disabilities costs money in the short term. However, the benefits of mainstreaming in the long term are tremendous, in both human and economic terms. After all, it is also very costly to keep children with disabilities in special schools and institutions. Some experts have estimated that it costs half a million dollars to keep one person in an institution for a lifetime. If, in contrast, children with disabilities can be mainstreamed into regular classrooms, taxpayers could save money over many years. Although it is impossible to measure the human costs of segregating persons with disabilities from mainstream schools, it makes sense to help persons with disabilities become as educated, productive, and independent as they possibly can. In this way, they not only realize their full right to education and employment, but also contribute to society.

The challenge of mainstreaming is not impossible. In order for mainstreaming to be effective, however, teachers and students must be properly trained. Teachers must be able to teach with the special needs of persons with disabilities in mind. Persons with disabilities must be prepared psychologically and physically to switch to regular schools. Schools must be prepared to commit resources and personnel to assist with individualized instruction. With the proper planning and cooperation between teachers, parents, and students, mainstreaming can benefit all persons in American society.

Disability rights legislation such as the Rehab Act, the EAHCA (now called IDEA), and the ADA all seek to mainstream persons with disabilities wherever practical and appropriate. These laws go far toward helping to realize the right to respect and education of all persons with disabilities.

Chapter Seven

The Right
to
Earn a Living

The President's Committee for Employment of People with Disabilities calculates that two-thirds of the nation's estimated 43 million disabled adults are unemployed. More than ninety percent of persons with *severe* disabilities are unemployed. The number of persons with disabilities living below the poverty level is at least twice as high as the able-bodied population. The vast majority receive some form of public assistance.

Barriers to Work

Discrimination against persons with disabilities in the work force has been common. Persons with disabilities are often hired for low-level, minimum-pay jobs that are frequently terminated on short notice. Employers who do hire persons with disabilities tend to promote them to more higher-paying and more responsible jobs less often than other workers. Employers have in the past tended to see and judge applicants with disabilities more on the basis of their disability than on the basis of their ability. Employer attitudes have in the past been less favorable to persons with disabilities than to elderly individuals, minority-group members, and ex-convicts.

"I DIDN'T KNOW YOU
WERE A *DISABLED VET!*"

Employers have often been unwilling to consider any blind or
mentally impaired person for any job. Far too often an
employer fails to have good information on the person. The
employer does not know how well the person is overcoming his
or her disability, what special training he or she has had, or
how motivated the person is. Employers tend to make
judgments on the basis of the disability alone.

Employers tend to believe that hiring a person with a
disability will cause their insurance rates to rise. In fact,
however, insurance companies have become leaders in
rehabilitating and hiring persons with disabilities. Insurance
rates do not automatically go up when persons with disabilities
are hired. Likewise, some employers wrongly believe that there
is a higher injury rate among persons with disabilities than
there is among able-bodied workers. They also believe that
persons with disabilities cannot work as well as able-bodied
persons. In 1948, the Department of Labor (DOL) conducted

an important study, *The Performance of Physically Impaired Workers in Manufacturing Industries.* This study revealed that there were no significant differences between persons with disabilities and able-bodied persons with respect to their productivity, injury rates, absences from work, and voluntary resignations. More recent statistics show that "impaired persons" actually have fewer disabling injuries than the average worker exposed to the same work hazards.

Many employers worry that costly physical adjustments will have to be made at the workplace to accommodate a worker with a disability. In 1973, E. I. du Pont de Nemours and Company conducted a survey of 1,452 of the company's employees with physical disabilities. They discovered that most employees required no special work arrangements. Moreover, the study found that 93 percent of its workers with disabilities rated average or better than other workers when it came to job stability.

Workers with disabilities also face certain types of procedural barriers. Labor contracts and job descriptions often require job applicants to perform tasks that, in fact, they will seldom or never be asked to do. Recent federal and state legislation rights laws relating to equal employment opportunity, affirmative action, and fair employment practices have helped to break down some of the procedural barriers.

While it is true that a person's disability might make job performance in certain areas impossible, the main problem is overcoming the barriers of attitude that block the right of persons with disabilities to get a job in the first place. In this respect, a distinction between a "disability" and a "handicap" must be made. A person may have a bodily, physiological, or psychological disability, but this does not necessarily mean that that person has a job-related "handicap." For example, a person with an amputated limb or a paralysis may or may not be able to do a particular job. A severely mobility-impaired

(Reprinted by permission of Boeing Corporation and the artist, John Fretz)

person may have no difficulty giving a lecture or teaching a class. What is "handicapping" the person with a disability is often the attitude of employers. Research data suggest that most persons with disabilities are an asset to their companies.

Vocational Rehabilitation

"Vocational rehabilitation" is a term that refers to any service that will help persons with disabilities get a job. Vocational rehabilitation offices are found in most cities. In many states, there are two rehabilitation agencies, one for blind persons and the other for persons with any other type of disability. In other states, a single rehabilitation agency serves all persons with disabilities. Vocational rehabilitation services vary from state to state, but certain services must be offered by every office, without charge and regardless of income. These rehabilitation services may involve counseling, testing, job training, guidance and referral services, job placement, and post-employment follow-up services. A person skilled in providing such services is known as a "vocational rehabilitation counselor" or simply a "rehabilitation counselor."

Federal and state vocational rehabilitation programs originated in the National Civilian Rehabilitation Act of 1920. Major revisions to that act were made in 1954, when the act was renamed the Vocational Rehabilitation Act. Since 1978, the U.S. Department of Education (DOE) has been responsible for overseeing vocational rehabilitation services. The Bureau of Education for the Handicapped provides money to public or nonprofit organizations and to state agencies for training rehabilitation personnel, constructing rehabilitation facilities, and funding research into new concepts of rehabilitation.

Vocational Rehabilitation for Disabled Veterans is a program run by the Veterans Administration. It trains veterans who acquired disabilities as a consequence of military service. The program provides up to four years of training and includes the entire cost of tuition, books, fees, and other supplies for school or training.

Other organizations — including the Easter Seal centers, Goodwill Industries, and a wide variety of mental health groups — offer vocational rehabilitation training programs and job development. A good example is the Training and Placement Service project (TAPS) of the Epilepsy Foundation of America.

The National Association of Retarded Citizens has an on-the-job training program that operates in forty-eight states. Some training centers charge fees adjusted to the client's income. Many organizations provide on-the-job experience in either sheltered or accommodated employment.

Sheltered and Accommodated Employment

Among vocational rehabilitation programs, *sheltered employment* refers to employment that does not require the worker to meet ordinary performance expectations. Often the quantity and quality of the work may be less than expected in other situations.

Accommodated employment, in contrast, does not relax work standards or expectations in any way. Rather, the term designates employment in which adjustments and adaptations to the environment are made in order to allow a person with disabilities to meet ordinary work standards and quantity. An "accommodation" might be physical, such as the installation of special drawers in a desk or a rampway leading into the office building. Another type of accommodation is a procedural one. An employer might allow a person with disabilities to maintain a flexible schedule. Those who work in vocational rehabilitation attempt to maximize the degree of accommodation that employers offer to persons with disabilities.

Public Attitudes Toward Persons With Disabilities

In 1991, Louis Harris and Associates conducted the first survey ever of American attitudes about persons with disabilities for the National Organization on Disability. The survey showed that Americans basically understand the many challenges persons with disabilities face in trying to earn a living and leading active lives as citizens, and that young Americans and those with a higher degree of education tend, more than others, to support persons with disabilities.

Public Attitudes   **Percentage**

Believe that persons with disabilities are not hired because of their disability.

Believe that persons with disabilities are not fully using their potential.

Believe that employment of persons with disabilities would be a great "boost" to the United States.

Believe that more spending is needed to make schools, transportation, workplaces, and other public buildings accessible.

Persons with disabilities who believe that they have been discriminated against in their efforts to find a job and to provide financially for themselves and their families.

Unemployed men with disabilities at the beginning of 1990 (according to the United States Attorney General).

Unemployed women with disabilities at the beginning of 1990 (according to the United States Attorney General).

The Need for Fair Standards

For most of the twentieth century, the employment of persons with mental disabilities has come from the residential institutions in which they were segregated from the mainstream of society. Under the name of "therapy," patients have often been forced to work without pay at cleaning, laundering, dishwashing, and housekeeping. In some cases, work assignments have been used as punishment.

In 1970, two mentally retarded youths charged that they had been forced to wash walls for more than ten consecutive hours on several occasions. Their class-action suit, *Wyatt v. Stickney*, was brought to court on behalf of all mentally ill and mentally retarded persons involuntarily confined in institutions in the state of Alabama. The suit was primarily concerned with the right to proper treatment. However, the court also ruled that patients in the institution could voluntarily engage in work if the work were fairly compensated in accordance with the minimum wage laws of the 1938 Fair Labor Standards Act. The ruling went on to distinguish between work that was "therapeutic," and thus part of treatment, and work that was "nontherapeutic," and thus deserving of payment.

The Rehabilitation Act of 1973

One of the most important job rights is contained within the Rehabilitation Act of 1973. Section 501 requires all federal agencies to take "affirmative action" in the hiring of qualified employees with disabilities. The idea behind this section of the act is that the federal government ought to be a model employer. The government, in other words, ought to set a positive example for the rest of the country in hiring persons with disabilities.

Section 501 goes beyond merely outlawing discrimination against persons with disabilities. Federal agencies must actively seek qualified applicants, make necessary accommodations for them in the workplace, offer them on-the-job training in order to assist them in the advancement of their profession, and make every good-faith effort to assist a person with a disability in retaining his or her job. Section 503 requires nondiscriminatory, affirmative-action hiring of qualified persons with disabilities for anyone having federal contracts of $2,500 or more. This is the most effectively enforced section of the act. Section 504 of the Rehab Act prohibits discrimination against individuals by any program or activity receiving federal funds. According to this section, it is necessary to make reasonable accommodations to make it possible for qualified persons with a disability to perform the job. This section also requires nondiscrimination in determining who receives job-related fringe benefits and privileges.

Employment and the ADA

Title I of the Americans with Disabilities Act of 1990 concerns employment rights for persons with disabilities. Title I states that employers may not discriminate in hiring or promotionagainst an individual with a disability if the person is otherwise qualified for the job. Employers may ask about one's ability to perform a job, but they cannot ask if one has a disability. They may not subject a person to tests that tend to screen out persons with disabilities. Employers are required to provide "reasonable accommodation" to persons with disabilities. This might include physical accessibility, acquiring special devices or modifying existing equipment, restructuring jobs, modifying schedules, or providing readers or interpreters. An example of reasonable accommodation might be exchanging a typist's telephone duties for other duties in order to allow a deaf person to hold that job.

Employers are not required to provide accommodations that impose an "undue hardship" on business operations.

Persons Aged 16-64 with a Work Disability, by State

States where the proportion of persons aged 16-64 with *work disabilities* is the highest are concentrated in the southern United States. The top 10 in percentage of disabled working age persons are: 1) Arkansas (12.7%); 2) West Virginia (12.3%); 3) Mississippi (11.8%); 4) Kentucky (11.4%); 5) Oklahoma (10.8%); 6) Alabama (10.6%); 7) Georgia and Tennessee (10.4%); and 9) Florida, Oregon, and District of Columbia (9.9%). The lowest proportions are: 51) Alaska (5.4%); 50) Hawaii (5.9%); 49) Wyoming (6.1%); 48) Connecticut (6.5%); 47) North Dakota (6.7%); 46) Wisconsin (6.8%); 45) New Jersey (6.9%); 44) Nebraska and Minnesota (7.0%); and 42) Iowa and Colorado (7.2%). Numbers of people with a work disability range from 1.3 million in California to 15,000 in Alaska.

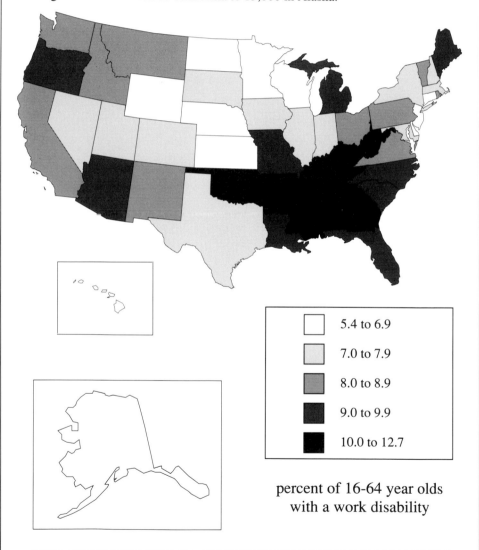

Legend:
- 5.4 to 6.9
- 7.0 to 7.9
- 8.0 to 8.9
- 9.0 to 9.9
- 10.0 to 12.7

percent of 16-64 year olds with a work disability

SOURCE: Reprinted with permission from L. Kraus and S. Stoddard, *Chartbook on Disability in the United States.* An InfoUse Report. Washington, D.C.: U.S. National Institute on Disability and Rehabilitation Research, 1989. Data are from the United States Census, 1980.

Employers may reject applicants or fire employees who pose a direct threat to the health or safety of other individuals in the workplace. Moreover, applicants and employees who are current drug users have no rights to claim discrimination on the basis of their illegal drug use under the ADA. Drug testing is not prohibited by the ADA. Employers may not discriminate against a qualified applicant or employee because of the known disability of an individual with whom the applicant or employee has a relationship or association. Furthermore, religious organizations may give preference in employment to their own members and may require applicants and employees to conform to their religious tenets.

Complaints concerning violations of the provisions of the ADA may be filed with the U.S. Equal Employment Opportunity Commission.

Chapter Eight

People Who Made a Difference

Persons with disabilities have been recognized leaders in their professional fields. Others have been leaders in the field of disability rights. Some of these persons are more famous than others. Some leaders have been previously mentioned in this book.

Louis Braille:
Inventor and Musician

Louis Braille was born in 1809, the son of a harness maker of the village of Coupvray outside Paris. At the age of three, he accidentally drove a small pricking tool into his left eye. In a few weeks he was blind in both eyes. There were usually only two options for blind children at that time: to be trained as a professional beggar or to shovel coal in a factory. Louis, however, attended the village school with sighted children until he was ten. Just by listening to the teacher, he was able to learn and perform better than his classmates. His father then enrolled him in the Institution Nationale des Jeunes, which had three large books in its library. The contents of these books were engraved in large, embossed letters (letters raised from the surface), and from these he learned to read. He was a bright student and a talented pianist and organist as well.

In order to develop a simpler system of writing for the blind, the young Braille drew upon the device of "night writing," which had been invented by an artillery captain named Charles Barbier. Barbier's system used dots and dashes that were embossed on something and so could be felt by the fingers. Braille discarded this system for a simpler pattern of two dots across and three dots down. He eventually devised sixty-three separate combinations of dots, representing all the letters in the French alphabet, as well as accents, punctuation marks, and mathematical signs.

Braille's ingenious system was not accepted at first, but it was eventually adopted all over France and throughout the world. He died on January 6, 1852, from tuberculosis.

Helen Keller:
A Spectacular Achievement

Helen Adams Keller was born in Tuscumbia, Alabama, on June 27, 1880. In February of 1882, she fell ill and was diagnosed as having "brain fever." The doctor thought that she would not survive. When the fever left her, nobody realized at first that she would never see or hear again. However, as the months passed, it became clear to her parents that Helen would never regain these abilities. They lost hope of raising her to live a normal life and allowed her to grow up wild and unruly. Helen's father, Captain Arthur Keller, was determined to educate Helen if at all possible. He took her to meet Dr. Alexander Graham Bell in Washington. Dr. Bell suggested that they write to the Perkins Institution for the Blind in Boston.

On March 3, 1887, Anne Mansfield Sullivan, a girl of twenty, arrived in Tuscumbia from the Perkins Institution to educate Helen Keller. Using special motions of her fingers, Anne Sullivan "spelled" into Helen's hand the words for all the things they did and all the objects with which Helen came into contact. After three years of instruction, Helen Keller knew the

Before she was two years old, Helen Keller lost the ability to see and hear. (Library of Congress)

alphabet, both manual and Braille, and could read and write. By this time, Helen had her own special name for the person who spelled into her hand: Teacher.

In June, 1904, Helen received her university degree (B.A. *cum laude*) from Radcliffe College with special mention of her excellence in English literature. She had learned to type, was proficient in French and German, and had made a special study of philosophy. "Teacher" and Helen Keller then moved to Wrentham, outside Boston. Keller then began to study the problems of the blind. Blind adults at that time were in desperate need of educational help and financial assistance. Because of her desire for justice for all people, Keller joined the Socialist party in 1909.

In 1908, Helen Keller was appointed to the Massachusetts State Commission for the Blind, and she began to write articles on blindness in the newborn and its prevention. In 1924, she began to raise funds for the American Foundation for the Blind and its information and science programs. She won numerous awards and honors and became known as one of the world's great social reformers. She is known for her willpower, courage, and the spectacular achievement of her life as a whole. Her sacrifices to improve the condition of the blind, in the face of her own disabilities, became an inspiration to all persons.

Keller died on June 1, 1968. Her body is buried at St. Joseph's Chapel in Washington Cathedral, Washington, D.C. She left behind her more than a dozen books, most famous of which include *The Story of My Life* (1902), *Optimism* (1903), *The World I Live In*, (1908), *Out of the Dark* (1913), *Midstream: My Later Life* (1930), *Helen Keller's Journal* (1938), *Let Us Have Faith* (1941), *Teacher* (1956), and *The Open Door* (1957). A film, *The Miracle Worker* (1962), based on her book *Teacher* and starring Patty Duke, received several awards.

Stephen Hawking:
Einstein's Rival

Stephen W. Hawking was born January 8, 1942, in Oxford, England. Before he was ten years old, he decided to become a scientist, since he enjoyed taking things apart. He completed his studies in physics at St. Albans School with top grades, and then entered Cambridge University. During his final year as a student there, he married Jane Wilde. Shortly thereafter, he finished his doctoral thesis.

Hawking did all this despite a severe physical impairment. He is almost totally paralyzed from Lou Gehrig's disease ("amyotrophic lateral sclerosis," or ALS). He must be fed by a nurse. He uses a computerized voice synthesizer to speak to others. He is also one of the world's most respected physicists and teaches at Cambridge University. He cannot write or type words or mathematical formulas. As a result, he must keep complicated mathematical equations in his mind. Some writers compare him to the musical composer Ludwig van Beethoven, who composed an entire symphony in his head despite encroaching deafness.

Despite his physical disability, Professor Hawking conducts lectures, writes books, and continues his physics research. He is attempting to explain the origin of the universe through his research on "black holes" (intensely compacted areas in the universe that collapsed under the weight of their own gravity). Most scientists now believe that black holes are not just theoretical but actually exist. The universe, which had a definite beginning, may have begun as an exploding black hole. It may someday end as a black hole too. Professor Hawking admits that science may never be able to understand or predict the behavior of the universe (the "principle of ignorance").

Many scientists consider Stephen Hawking to be the most creative mind in physics since Albert Einstein. He has received

Stephen Hawking, physicist. (Miriam Berkley)

numerous science awards and honors. He also is father to three children. He never works at home, but he gives his children as much time as he can. It is a major credit to the man — and to the human spirit — that he earned his doctorate in physics and accomplished more by age fifty than most people do in a lifetime, despite one of the most debilitating physical impairments known.

Eunice K. Fiorito:
Disability Rights Leader

Eunice K. Fiorito was born Eunice K. Frelly on October 1, 1930, in Chicago. She was diagnosed as blind at eight months of age due to an overdose of silver nitrate in the eyes at birth. While she regained her vision after the removal of cataracts at the age of three, she later lost her vision permanently at the age of sixteen. In turn, she virtually mastered the difficult art of reading and writing Braille in only two weeks' time.

Fiorito's first job was working with the Chicago Lighthouse for the Blind. She earned five cents per hour putting together wires for telephones. She eventually organized the workers to speak out against an unjust system. This was the beginning of what would prove to be much experience with discrimination.

In 1954, she earned a degree in education from Loyola University of Chicago. She then worked as a counselor and rehabilitation teacher at the Illinois State Department of Public Welfare. Her work was to provide home instruction in mobility skills for newly blinded individuals and to provide counseling and community resources. She went on to earn another degree (a master's degree in social work) and established one of the first psychiatric social work programs for blind persons in the nation at Roosevelt Hospital and the Jewish Guild for the Blind in New York.

Through her social work, Eunice Fiorito came to believe that the solutions to many of the problems faced by persons with disabilities are political ones. In 1974, she helped found and became the first president of the American Coalition of Citizens with Disabilities (ACCD). The ACCD is dedicated to the human and civil rights of persons with disabilities. Its focus is not on helping individual persons with disabilities directly. Rather, it focuses on achieving its goals through shaping government social policy via disability rights legislation.

Eunice Fiorito believes that changing society's perceptions of persons with disabilities requires government advocacy. She is one of the most outspoken advocates in the history of the disability rights movement. The government, according to Fiorito, ought to ensure the rights of and provide services to persons with disabilities. She also believes that persons with disabilities need to work with other minority groups in the struggle for human and civil rights. Eunice Fiorito is a woman who practices what she preaches.

Jean Vanier:
Founder of L'Arche Communities

Jean Vanier was born in 1928 in Canada. He joined the Canadian Royal Navy at age thirteen and spent nine years in the Navy. Afterward, he spent more than a decade studying Roman Catholic philosophy and theology. In August of 1964, at the age of thirty-five, he bought a house in the French village of Trosly, northeast of Paris. He arranged for two mentally impaired persons to live with him, thus beginning his ministry to persons with mental disabilities.

The key to Vanier's work with the mentally retarded is his conviction that persons with mental disabilities are often more open to spiritual values such as kindness and love than are other persons. Today, about two hundred mentally impaired persons live in twenty-one houses in Trosly and nearby villages, along with their personal care assistants. These are L'Arche, or "The Ark," communities. Worldwide, L'Arche has ninety-five communities in twenty-two countries as diverse as Haiti, India, and the Ivory Coast. There are twenty-four L'Arche communities in Canada. Many who volunteer as personal care assistants in L'Arche communities share Vanier's religious faith and remain celibate in order to deepen their relationship with God.

In 1980, Vanier stepped down as director of the L'Arche communities. He continued to spend about half of his time traveling on behalf of the organization he had founded. In 1989, Jean Vanier received the Order of Canada award for his twenty-five years of work with mentally retarded persons. In the early 1990's, he began to concentrate on establishing L'Arche communities in the countries of the former Soviet Union and post-Communist Eastern European countries.

Judy Heumann:
Disability Rights Activist

Judy Heumann's paraplegia was the result of polio. She never learned to walk, requiring the aid of a wheelchair. Despite her disability, she was graduated from Long Island University in 1969. She wanted to teach school, but after her graduation, education authorities would not allow her to teach. Even though she was well qualified to be a teacher, she was told that she had failed the physical examination because of the paralysis of her legs.

Heumann filed a lawsuit against the school board. She was finally allowed to teach. She also founded a group called the Disabled in Action, which fought for the rights of persons with disabilities.

Edward Roberts:
Independent Living Initiator

Edward Roberts came down with polio in 1953. He was fourteen years old at the time, a likable youth, an athlete, and a leader. His polio left him paralyzed below the neck. He became a mobility-impaired quadriplegic who had to spend much time in an iron lung to help him breathe.

Roberts recovered sufficiently from polio to earn two degrees from the University of California at Berkeley. In 1972 he, along with Judy Heumann, founded the Center for Independent Living (CIL) in Berkeley, California. The center provides a range of services such as peer counseling, legal services, van transportation, training in independent living skills, attendant care referral, health maintenance, housing referral, and wheelchair repair.

Evan J. Kemp:
Equal Opportunity Advocate

Evan J. Kemp, Jr., has been a longtime worker in the disability rights movement. He has a muscle and nerve disability and is mobility-impaired. In March, 1989, Kemp became chairman of the Equal Employment Opportunity Commission (EEOC). He has won the praise of civil rights activists for his work against discrimination by employers. He has initiated numerous high-profile lawsuit and policy decisions and has worked hard to stop employment discrimination.

Kemp knows what job discrimination is like from his own experience. In the mid-1960's, he was rejected by thirty-nine law firms. In 1979, he won a lawsuit against the Securities & Exchange Commission. The commission refused to promote him, because he uses a wheelchair. As a member of the EEOC, he helped win government support for the 1990 Americans with Disabilities Act (ADA).

Chapter Nine

Access to
the Future

Great strides have been made in the past two decades toward
enacting and enforcing disability rights legislation in the
United States and around the world. In many respects, persons
with disabilities are much more able to realize their full human
dignity and rights as persons today than ever before in history.

Yet, much work remains to be done before persons with
disabilities will receive "equal access" in the full sense of that
term: both physically and socially. Six out of every ten persons
with disabilities around the world are not receiving basic
health care, special education, vocational rehabilitation, or job
placement services. It takes time before disability rights
legislation becomes more than an abstract law and is fully
implemented.

For example, the Architectural Barriers Act of 1968 required
that any building leased, owned, or constructed with federal
funds be accessible to, and usable by, persons with disabilities
according to specified government standards. Today, far too
many buildings still are functionally inaccessible to persons
with disabilities. The Education for All Handicapped Children
Act was passed in 1975. However, too few persons with
disabilities have benefitted from educational programs that
truly prepare them to earn a living for themselves and their
loved ones.

The Promise of the ADA

The passage of the Americans with Disabilities Act in 1990 established by law the rights of persons with disabilities to equal and full employment opportunities, equal access, public accommodations, and telecommunications services.

The ADA is the most significant disability rights act of the twentieth century. However, vigorous leadership by federal, state, and local governments will be required to implement the legislation and its programs of service. The implementation of the ADA and disability rights rests on the concerned attitudes of every person in the United States. The promise of the ADA for the future is great, but so is the challenge of its full implementation.

Defending Persons with Mental Disabilities

At least sixty million Americans between the ages of eighteen and sixty-four will experience a mental disorder during their lifetime. The Americans with Disabilities Act forbids employers from asking job applicants whether they have a history of mental illness. Most American states have laws protecting persons with physical disabilities. Yet, many laws do not include protections for persons with mental or emotional disabilities.

Drug and alcohol problems affect about 27 million people of working age in the United States. Some 15 million adults will experience one or more of three types of severe mental illness such as schizophrenia, manic-depressive disorders, or major depression in their lifetimes. One of four Americans will experience a disability, such as claustrophobia, personality problems, or mental retardation.

The disability rights movement must in the future expand its reach to include greater solidarity with persons with emotional or mental disabilities in the years ahead. As the ADA begins to take effect, it will be an important tool for defending the rights of persons with mental disabilities. The act cannot entirely overcome the widespread and deep-seated fear and hostility toward any kind of mental illness. The ADA is, however, a truly remarkable start in the right direction.

Personal Assistant Services

Personal assistant services are yet another vital means of helping Americans with disabilities to realize their right to achieve their full potential as productive members of society in the future. Government officials estimate that excluding two-thirds of Americans with disabilities from the mainstream costs Americans $200 billion per year. Providing public and private personal assistant services to those with disabilities pays off in the long term. It costs far less to provide personal assistant services than traditional medical services, institutionalization, or social welfare. More important, there is usually an improved quality of life for both the recipient and the provider by means of such services. In general, many Americans spend enormous amounts of money on luxury automobiles, recreation, and other excessive material goods. A society cannot morally do this when millions of persons with disabilities are deprived of basic personal care services.

Disability Rights and the Global Village

What is the future outlook of rights for persons with disabilities around the world?

In 1975, the General Assembly of the United Nations adopted a Declaration on the Rights of Disabled Persons. The Declaration named the inherent right to respect for the human dignity of persons with disabilities, and noted that they have the very same civil and political rights as other human beings. The United Cerebral Palsy Association has also defined disability rights. UCPA issued a Bill of Rights for the Handicapped following the purposes and concerns of the

American Bill of Rights. Their identification of disability rights is similar to the rights set forth by the United Nations.

The year 1981 was the International Year of Disabled Persons (IYDP). Its theme was "full participation" and "equality." The first means the right of persons with disabilities to take part fully in the life and development of their societies. It means persons with disabilities have a right to enjoy living conditions similar to those of other citizens in society. It means that they have a right, by law, to equal access to and a share in improved conditions resulting from socioeconomic development.

Canada has conducted a survey of persons with disabilities in recent years. In 1987, it was estimated that almost 14 percent of the entire Canadian population had limitations getting around inside and outside the home, speaking, hearing, seeing, ascending stairs, lifting, and walking.

In 1992, more than 500 million human beings living on the planet were impaired as a consequence of mental, physical, or sensory disabilities. Eighty percent of these people live in isolated rural areas in Third World countries. Because of the physical and social barriers in society which hamper their full participation, millions of children and adults still suffer a life that is segregated, debased, and in violation of their basic human rights and access to equal opportunity. Grinding poverty is a harsh reality for most persons with disabilities around the world. Fewer than one in ten of these 500 million persons are protected in any significant way from discrimination.

Full Participation and Equal Access

All disability rights legislation is only as powerful and effective as the people who support and guard the laws. Laws alone cannot establish human rights. Only people actively working on behalf of persons with disabilities will bring about integration of persons with disabilities into the economic and social mainstream of society. Economic and social integration is perhaps the most important key to full respect and full participation for persons with disabilities.

Now is the time to move history forward toward the full participation and equality of persons with disabilities. Persons with disabilities are persons with abilities, persons who command respect flowing from their human dignity. The disability rights legislation discussed in this book reveals that the discrimination and neglect of persons with disabilities can and must become a thing of the past. Recent polls and legal developments promise a positive outlook for persons with disabilities and the fuller implementation of their human rights.

George Bush signing the Americans with Disabilities Act into law. Standing, left to right: the Reverend Harold Wilkie and Sandra Parrino, National Council on Disability. Seated, left to right: Evan Kemp, Chair, Equal Employment Opportunity Commission; President Bush; Justin Dart, Chair, President's Committee on the Employment of People with Disabilities. (Joyce Naltchayam/Courtesy The White House)

Time Line

1918   The Soldiers Rehabilitation Act is passed, allowing the Federal
         Board for Vocational Education to rehabilitate disabled veterans.
1918   Congress passes the first Vocational Rehabilitation Act.
1920   The National Civilian Rehabilitation Act is early legislation
         providing for vocational rehabilitation programs at the federal and
         state levels.
1935   Congress passes the Social Security Act, which establishes
         unemployment compensation and old-age retirement insurance.
1946   The Social Security Administration considers a person "disabled" if
         he or she is blind or has an impairment that makes it impossible to
         work.
1947   The President's Committee on Employment of the Handicapped is
         established.
1949   The Housing Act (P.L. 81-171) makes persons with disabilities
         eligible for inclusion in projects sponsored by the Department of
         Housing and Urban Development.
1954   The Vocational Rehabilitation Act (formerly the National Civilian
         Rehabilitation Act) passes Congress.
1956   Social Security Disability Insurance is created by the government to
         help persons with total disabilities.
1959   The President's Committee on Employment of the Handicapped and
         the National Easter Seal Society for Crippled Children and Adults
         launch the first nationwide campaign to eliminate architectural
         barriers.
1961   The American National Standards Institute (ANSI) publishes its
         *Specifications for Making Buildings and Facilities Accessible to, and
         Usable by, the Physically Handicapped.*
1963   The Mental Retardation Facilities and Community Mental Health
         Centers Construction Act of 1963, (P.L. 88-164) is passed.
1965   The Elementary and Secondary Education Act is passed; it
         establishes the right of "disabled" children to educational services.
1965   The Housing and Urban Development Act (P.L. 89-117) expands the
         government's financial commitment to provide rent subsidies to the
         "handicapped" and the elderly.

1965 Congress passes the Vocational Rehabilitation Amendments, creating a National Commission on Architectural Barriers to the Rehabilitation of the Handicapped.

1967 The Social and Rehabilitation Service unites welfare, vocational rehabilitation, and other social services into one large federal agency.

1967 The Helen Keller National Center for Deaf-Blind Youths and Adults is established by congressional mandate.

1968 The Architectural Barriers Act (ABA) requires that any building leased, owned, or constructed with federal funds be accessible to, and usable by, persons with disabilities according to specified government standards.

1968 The Joseph P. Kennedy, Jr., Foundation establishes the Special Olympics.

1969 Congress passes the Education of the Handicapped Act (P.L. 91-230).

1972 The Rehabilitation Services Administration is created within the Department of Health, Education, and Welfare, starting a new program of independent living services for persons with severe disabilities.

1973 The Rehabilitation Act is passed, providing the basic federal law containing programs and rights for persons with disabilities.

1973 The Federal-Aid Highway Act (P.L. 93-87) requires that certain highways and roads be made accessible to those with disabilities.

1974 The Housing and Community Development Act (P.L. 93-383) provides financial subsidies for alternative living arrangements for persons with disabilities.

1975 The Education of All Handicapped Children Act (EAHCA), P.L. 94-142, is passed, requiring a "free appropriate public education" and an "individualized education program" to all children with disabilities aged three to twenty-one.

1975 The United Nations General Assembly adopts its Declaration on the Rights of Disabled Persons.

1981 The United Nations Year of Disabled Persons implements worldwide programs to promote full participation and equality of persons with disabilities.

1983 The National Council on the Handicapped issues its National Policy for Persons with Disabilities.

1984 The Voting Accessibility for the Elderly and Handicapped Act passes Congress.

1986   The Air Carriers Access Act prohibits commercial airlines from discriminating against persons with disabilities in the provision of transportation services.

1988   Congress passes the Civil Rights Restoration Act. Qualified persons with disabilities must be given the same opportunities as able-bodied colleagues in all phases of employment.

1990   The 1975 Education for All Handicapped Children Act (EAHCA) is renamed the Individuals with Disabilities Education Act (IDEA), P.L. 101-476.

1990   The Americans with Disabilities Act provides civil rights protection for persons with disabilities, including provisions for employment, state and local government services, public accommodations, transportation, and the telephone system.

1991   Louis Harris and Associates publish the first study ever of how Americans view persons with disabilities.

Publications

Books for Young Readers

Aaseng, Nathan. *Bruce Jenner: Decathlon Winner*. Minneapolis: Lerner Publications, 1979. A biography of the young American with dyslexia whose four years of intense training enabled him to win the decathlon at the 1976 Olympics in Montreal, Canada.

Baron, Connie. *The Physically Disabled*. Edited by Maythee Kantar. Mankato, Minn.: Crestwood House, 1988. Discusses various diseases and conditions that can cause physical disabilities.

Dick, Jean. *Mental and Emotional Disabilities*. Edited by Maythee Kantar. Mankato, Minn.: Crestwood House, 1988. Discusses autism, depression, mental retardation, dyslexia, stuttering, hyperactivity, and other mental and emotional disabilities.

Eagles, Douglas A. *The Menace of AIDS: A Shadow on Our Land*. New York: Franklin Watts, 1988. Discusses the origins, causes, characteristics, methods of infection, possible cures and prevention, and social aspects of the deadly disease.

Gravelle, Karen. *Understanding Birth Defects*. New York: Franklin Watts, 1990. Examines the causes of birth defects, the hardships faced by children born with them, and the ways of preventing them.

Hyde, Margaret O. *Is This Kid "Crazy"? Understanding Unusual Behavior*. Philadelphia: Westminster Press, 1983. An interesting and practical guide for those who want facts about problems of mental disabilities and other unusual behaviors.

Keeler, Stephen. *Louis Braille*. New York: Bookwright Press, 1986. An excellent late elementary and middle school introduction to the person and life of Braille.

Knox, Jean McBee. *Learning Disabilities*. Introduction by C. Everett Koop. New York: Chelsea House, 1989. Discusses the nature, possible causes, and treatment of learning disabilities, how they are diagnosed, and whom they affect.

Meyer, Donald J., Patricia F. Vadasy, and R. Fewell. *Living with a Brother or Sister with Special Needs: A Book for Sibs*. Seattle: University of Washington Press, 1985. Written for siblings of children with special needs, this book is an excellent resource for middle school students.

Rosenberg, Maxine B. *Finding a Way: Living with Exceptional Brothers and Sisters*. New York: Lothrop, Lee & Shepard Books, 1988. Numerous black-and-white photographs and text describe brother-sister relationships in which one sibling has a physical disability. Recommended for elementary students.

Wepman, Dennis. *Helen Keller*. American Women of Achievement Series. New York: Chelsea House, 1982. An excellent resource with fine photographs. Includes a chronology of Keller's life and an index.

Books for Adult Readers

Berkowitz, Edward D. *Disabled Policy: America's Programs for the Handicapped*. A Twentieth Century Fund Report. Cambridge, England: Cambridge University Press, 1987. A scholarly history of the politics of disability policy in the United States.

Bowe, Frank. *Handicapping America: Barriers to Disabled People*. New York: Harper & Row, 1978. The author is an internationally respected authority on disability.

Crawford, Irene. *Aids to Independence: A Guide to Products for the Disabled and the Elderly*. Vancouver, Toronto: International Self-Counsel Press, 1985. A practical guide to communication, mobility, and walking aids written to help senior citizens and persons with disabilities achieve greater independence.

Crewe, Nancy M., and Irving Kenneth Zola. *Independent Living for Physically Disabled People: Developing, Implementing, and Evaluating Self-Help Rehabilitation Programs*. San Francisco: Jossey-Bass, 1983. Written for people working in the field of independent living, professionals in the fields of vocational and medical rehabilitation, and students preparing careers in which they will be working with disabled persons.

Goldman, Charles. *Disability Rights Guide: Practical Solutions to Problems Affecting People with Disabilities*. 2d ed. Lincoln, Nebr.: Media Publishing, 1987, 1991. The author has been actively involved with disability rights and legislation since 1975.

Haskins, James, with J. M. Stifle. *The Quiet Revolution: The Struggle for the Rights of Disabled Americans*. New York: Thomas Y. Crowell, 1979. Focuses on the human and civil rights of persons with disabilities.

Katz, Alfred H., and Knute Martin. *A Handbook of Services for the Handicapped*. Westport, Conn.: Greenwood Press, 1982. A practical reference that emphasizes the common problems faced by persons with disabilities.

McWilliams, Peter A. *Personal Computers and the Disabled*. Garden City, N.Y.: Doubleday, 1984. An excellent resource accessible to the younger reader as well as the adult.

Resources for Rehabilitation. *Resources for People with Disabilities and Chronic Conditions*. Lexington, Mass.: Resources for Rehabilitation, 1991. A directory of rehabilitation resources to help persons with disabilities, the chronically ill, their families, and service providers.

Media Resources

Audiovisual Resources
Filmakers Library
124 East 40th St.
New York, NY 10016
(212) 808-4980

Modern Talking Picture Services
Captioned Films for the Deaf
5000 Park Street, N.
St. Petersburg, FL 33709
(800) 237-6213; (813) 541-7571

Perennial Education
930 Pitner Ave.
Evanston, IL 60202
(708) 328-6700; (800) 323-9084; FAX (708) 328-6706

Video Press
University of Maryland at Baltimore
School of Medicine
32 South Greene St.
Baltimore, MD 21201
(410) 328-7720

Videotapes and Films
Beginning with Bong. Video. Available from Video Press. Shot primarily on
location in mainstream elementary and middle schools, this program
documents medical information on arthrogryposis, spina bifida, spinal
cord injury, muscular dystrophy, and cerebral palsy.
Born on the Fourth of July. Film. Released by Universal, 1989. Widely
available on videotape. A dramatization of the story of a Vietnam War
veteran, paralyzed from the waist down, who turned antiwar activist:
Ron Kovic. Chronicles the emotional rehabilitation of a man who, like

many others of his generation and many who face similar disabilities, had to overcome not only physical challenges but attitudinal ones as well.

Children of a Lesser God. Film. Released by Paramount Pictures, 1986. Widely available on videotape. Starring Marlee Matlin, who is deaf in real life, the story of a deaf woman who falls in love with a hearing teacher for the deaf (William Hurt). This film used only hearing-impaired actors to portray similarly impaired characters, and American Sign Language is extensively employed.

Coma: The Journey Back. Video. Produced by Varied Directions. Available from Filmakers Library. Treats memory, locomotive skills, ability to reason, power of speech, awareness of reality, and quality of life issues.

Coming Home. Film. Released by United Artists, 1978. Available on videotape. Examines the effect of the Vietnam War on the lives and relationships of veterans with disabilities, including a paraplegic played by Jon Voight.

David: Portrait of a Retarded Youth. Video. Produced by Canadian Broadcasting Corporation. Available from Filmakers Library. Seeing David's determined efforts to master new situations and his success in many areas will inspire those who work or live with the mentally handicapped.

Dealing with Cancer: Tangled in a Threat. Video. Available from Perennial Education. For children with cancer, their families, and health care professionals.

A Friend Like You. Video. Available from Perennial Education. Encourages young children to befriend children with mental disabilities in the school, classroom, or community.

Home, Heart, Hope: Community Living for the Severely Mentally Retarded. Video. Directed by Phil Katzman. Available from Filmakers Library. A touching portrayal of the actual experiences of parents, siblings, and physically handicapped people.

Language Says It All: Communicating with the Hearing-Impaired Child. Video. Produced for Tripod Films by Megan Williams and Rhyena Halpern. Available from Filmakers Library. This Academy Award-nominated film explores the difficulties of bringing up a hearing-impaired child in a hearing family.

Learning Disabilities — First Hand. 16mm film. Available from Perennial Education. Provides viewers with a clear understanding of the social, emotional, and academic obstacles faced by students with learning disabilities.

Little People. Video. A film by Jan Krawitz and Thomas Ott. Available from Filmakers Library. A moving and sometimes funny documentary on the experience of being a dwarf among average-sized people.

The Miracle Worker. Film. Released by United Artists, 1962. Available on videotape. Anne Bancroft and Patty Duke both won Academy Awards for their portrayal, respectively, of Anne Sullivan ("Teacher") and Helen Keller, the renowned writer and lecturer who was born deaf and blind.

Mirror, Mirror. Video. Produced by Canadian Broadcasting Corporation. Available from Filmakers Library. Examines the lives of several people of various ages who go through life with facial disfigurement.

More than Enough: Literacy for the Hearing Impaired. Video. Produced by Canadian Broadcasting Corporation. Available from Filmakers Library. An advocacy film demanding that the hearing-impaired be given equal educational opportunity.

My Left Foot. Film. Released by Miramax Films, 1989. Widely available on videotape. Academy Award winner Daniel Day-Lewis portrays Christy Brown in this film based on his life. Despite severe cerebral palsy, Brown is able not only to write and paint but also to touch others with his wide range of feeling. The film is notable for being emotionally true rather than manipulative.

Nobody Is Burning Wheelchairs. Video. Produced by the National Easter Seal Society. Available from Administrative Services Department, National Easter Seal Society. Explains the Americans With Disabilities Act (ADA) provisions for equal access to employment, transportation,and telecommunications. Emphasizes the importance of seeing people with disabilities as *people*.

Rachael, Being Five. Video. Available from Video Press. Spans twelve months in the life of a child with cerebral palsy, capturing joys and challenges at home and school. Nominated for a CINE Golden Eagle for best achievement in children's programming, this program is appropriate for educators and health professionals and excellent for general audiences and elementary students.

Rain Man. Film. Released by United Artists, 1988. Widely available on videotape. Dustin Hoffman won an Academy Award for his portrayal of the middle-aged brother of a cynical young hustler. The sweetness of Hoffman's character shines through despite his severe autism, and ultimately the younger brother learns from him what it means to be human.

Riding the Gale. Video. A film by Genni and Kim Batterham. Available from Filmakers Library. When Genni learned she had multiple sclerosis, she feared for her marriage and her career. A film about a relationship in the face of disease.

Shakissha and Friends. Video. Available from Video Press. Documents the transfer of a ten-year-old girl with spina bifida from a school for handicapped children to a mainstream class. Excellent for a general audience, as well as elementary and middle school students.

The Vision of the Blind. Video. Produced by Canadian Broadcasting Corporation. Available from Filmakers Library. Shows both special and mainstreamed schools where young children gain the confidence and skills to lead fulfilling lives.

Walking on Air. Video. Produced by KCET/Los Angeles and "WonderWorks" Family Movie Series, 1986. Based on a story idea by the science-fiction writer Ray Bradbury. Excellent for a middle-school audience.

The World at His Fingertips. Video. Produced by Helen Keller, National Center for Deaf-Blind Youths and Adults. Available from Filmakers Library. A film about Mike Van Orman, married and the father of two sons, who lost both his sight and his hearing when he was in his thirties.

Television Series

L.A. Law. Larry Drake plays Benny Stulwicz, a mentally retarded man, who is a file clerk in the law firm.

Life Goes On. Chris Burke, an actor with Down syndrome in real life, plays Corky, a teenager with Down syndrome.

Reasonable Doubts. Marlee Matlin, a deaf actress and star of the movie *Children of a Lesser God*, plays a deaf prosecutor who works with a non-deaf investigator who knows sign language.

Workshop

Welcome to My World. Available from the Special Pastoral Services Department of the Archdiocese of Portland in Oregon. Simulates eight different disabilities. A valuable tool for raising disability awareness.

Organizations
and
Hotlines

Abledata Information System
426 W. Jefferson
Springfield, IL 62702
(217) 523-2587
(800) 526-0857
(800) 523-6304 (TDD)
(217) 523-0427 (FAX)
   An information and referral service for a wide variety of disabilities and disability-related matters, including agencies, education, employment, adaptive equipment, housing, funding and financial resources, law, personal care, recreation/travel, standards, statistics, and surveys.

American Council of the Blind
1155 15th St. NW, Suite 720
Washington, DC 20005
(202) 467-5081
(800) 424-8666
(202) 467-5085 (FAX)
   Promotes legislative and governmental advances that enhance the lives of blind or near-blind individuals.

The Arc (formerly Association for Retarded Citizens)
P.O. Box 300649
Arlington, TX 76010
(817) 261-6003
(817) 277-0553 (TDD)
   The primary U.S. advocacy group for children and adults with mental retardation: provides information about rights as well as prevention of mental retardation; advocates on the federal level.

Blinded Veterans Association
477 H St. NW
Washington, DC 20001
(202) 371-8880
(800) 669-7079
(202) 371-8258 (FAX)
Assists blinded veterans in overcoming educational, employment, and daily living problems.

Council for Exceptional Children
1920 Association Dr.
Reston, VA 22091
(703) 620-3660; for TDD, ext. 307
(800) 845-6232
(703) 264-9494 (FAX)
Conducts research and training on the education of children and youth with disabilities.

Disability Rights Center
2500 Q St. NW, Suite 121
Washington, DC 20007
(202) 337-4119
Advocates on behalf of disabled applicants and employees in an effort to secure full implementation of Section 501 of the Rehabilitation Act of 1973.

Epilepsy Foundation of America
4351 Garden City Dr.
Landover, MD 20785
(301) 459-3700
(800) EFA-1000
(301) 577-2684 (FAX)
Provides useful information on epilepsy, including information about various state laws concerning driving and epilepsy.

Equal Employment Opportunity Commission
1801 L St. NW
Washington, DC 20507
(202) 663-4900
(202) 663-4141 (TDD)
(202) 663-4110 (FAX)

Established by the Civil Rights Act of 1964, this agency sees that workers receive equal opportunities in hiring and on the job. There are EEOC branch offices across the nation.

Independent Living Research Utilization
2323 S. Shepherd, Suite 1000
Houston, TX 77019
(713) 520-0232
(713) 520-5136 (TDD)
ILRU is a national center for training, research, and technical assistance in, as well as information on, independent living.

March of Dimes Birth Defects Foundation
1275 Mamaroneck Ave.
White Plains, NY 10605
(914) 428-7100
(914) 428-8203 (FAX)
Works for the prevention of birth defects.

Muscular Dystrophy Associations of America, Inc.
3561 E. Sunrise Dr.
Tucson, AZ 85718
(602) 529-2000
(800) 223-6666
(602) 529-5300 (FAX)
Fosters research into cures and treatments for muscular dystrophy and related neuromuscular diseases.

National Association of the Deaf
814 Thayer Ave.
Silver Spring, MD 20910
(301) 587-1788 (voice and TDD)
Serves as a clearinghouse and advocacy group in matters relating to deafness and hearing impairment.

National Catholic Office for Persons with Disabilities
P.O. Box 29113
Washington, DC 20017
(202) 529-2933 (voice and TDD)
Promotes awareness about persons with disabilities within the Roman Catholic church. Provides resources on ministries to and persons with disabilities.

National Council on Disability
800 Independence Ave. SW, Suite 814
Washington, DC 20591
(202) 267-3846
(202) 267-3232 (TDD)
(202) 453-4240 (FAX)
Provides sources of information on legislation affecting persons with disabilities. Publishes *Focus*, in large print or on tape.

National Easter Seal Society
70 East Lake St.
Chicago, IL 60601
(312) 726-6200
(312) 726-4258 (TDD)
(312) 726-1494 (FAX)
A federation of local facilities serving disabled persons and their families.

National Multiple Sclerosis Society
733 Third Ave., Sixth Floor
New York, NY 10017
(212) 986-3240
(800) 624-8236 (tape)
(800) 227-3166 (hotline)
(212) 986-7981 (FAX)
Supports research on the central nervous system and educates persons about multiple sclerosis.

National Organization on Disability
910 Sixteenth St. NW, Suite 600
Washington, DC 20006
(202) 293-5960
(800) 248-2253
(202) 293-7999 (FAX)
Works to expand participation of persons with disabilities in society.

National Spinal Cord Injury Association
600 West Cummings Park, Suite 2000
Roburn, MA 01801
(617) 935-2722

(800) 962-9629
(617) 932-8369 (FAX)

Advocates for persons with spinal cord injuries. Promotes research, training, and treatment in the area of spinal cord injury.

Office on the Americans with Disabilities Act
Civil Rights Division
U.S. Department of Justice
P.O. Box 66118
Washington, DC 20035-6118
(202) 514-0301

Provides information on the ADA in an effort to support its national implementation.

Rehabilitation International
25 East 21st St.
New York, NY 10010
(212) 420-1500
(212) 505-0871 (FAX)

An organization, located in eighty-three nations, that conducts programs for the rehabilitation of persons with physical and mental disabilities.

Telecommunications for the Deaf, Inc.
8719 Colesville Rd.
Silver Spring, MD 20910
(301) 589-3786
(301) 589-3006 (TDD)
(301) 589-3797 (FAX)

Publishes a directory of TDD numbers to improve communication between deaf persons via telephone.

United Cerebral Palsy Associations, Inc.
7 Penn Plaza
New York, NY 10001
(212) 268-6655
(800) USA-1UCP
(212) 268-5960 (FAX)

Seeks solutions to the obstacles facing persons who have cerebral palsy.

INDEX